CAR...ON
TALKING

How Dead Are The Voices?

PETER BANDER

www.whitecrowbooks.com

Carry on Talking

For information, contact White Crow Books by
e-mail: info@whitecrowbooks.com.

Cover Design by Astrid@Astridpaints.com
Interior design by Velin@Perseus-Design.com

Paperback: ISBN: 978-1-78677-159-9
eBook: ISBN: 978-1-78677-160-5

Non-Fiction / Body, Mind & Spirit / Parapsychology
/ Afterlife & Reincarnation

www.whitecrowbooks.com

The Church and the Voices

"It is all very mysterious, but we know that the voices are there for everyone to hear."
~ *His Excellency Archbishop Cardinale, Apostolic Nuncio*

"I'm definitely impressed, and willing to be impressed by this phenomenon."
~ *The Rt. Rev. Dr. Butler, Anglican Bishop of Connor*

"The message these voices hold for me is confirmation that there is life after death."
~ *The Very Rev. Fr. Pistone, S.S.P.*

"It is a reality backed by experience and established by evidence open to all, that the dead live and can communicate with us."
~ *The Rt. Rev. Mgr. Prof. C. Pfleger*

The Scientists and the Voices

"I can no longer explain the voice phenomena in normal physical terms.
~ *Peter A. Hale, physicist*

"Extensive experiments have shown that the paranormal origin of the voices is highly probable."
~ *Prof. H. Bender, Director, University Institute of Psychology, Freiburg*

"I'm convinced that these are the voices of the dead."
~ *Robert Crookall, B. Sc (psychology), Ph.D., D.Sc*

"I have succeeded in reproducing the phenomenon. Voices which did not come from any known source have appeared on a tape."
~ *Dr. Brendan McGann, Director Institute of Psychology, Dublin*

BY THE SAME AUTHOR

One for the Road
Two for the Road
The Prophecies of St. Malachy
Off the Cuff
A Rose by any Other Name

(Editor)
Looking Forward to the Seventies
Eternal Youth and Music

To the memory of my friend
THE RT. REV. MGR. STEPHEN O'CONNOR
V.G., P.R.C.C., R.N.
whose last message to me before his death was
"You must talk about Breakthrough"

Contents

Introduction

Since 1959 a great number of scientists, electronics experts, psychologists and enthusiastic amateurs have been engaged in recording and analysing electronic Voice Phenomena which manifest themselves on ordinary electro-magnetic recording tape. After extensive research the theory was put forward that these might be the voices of people from beyond the grave.

In 1968 the Latvian psychologist Dr. Konstantin Raudive published his own research findings in Germany under the title *The Inaudible Becomes Audible*. At the Frankfurt Book Fair in October 1969 the English publisher Colin Smythe was given a copy of this book, which in turn, he handed to me for consideration. My first reaction to the book was negative because the claims made by the author appeared to me not only far-fetched but outrageous; although I knew some of Dr. Raudive's collaborators personally and have always respected their scientific work, the thought of dead people communicating through a tape recorder seemed ludicrous and too silly to be taken seriously.

My own position as a Senior Lecturer in Religious and Moral Education and as a trained psychologist may well have prejudiced me and I advised Colin Smythe against publication of the book in the English language. Unknown to me, he carried out an experiment according to the instructions given in Raudive's book which I had translated in parts in order to justify my decision. The first recording yielded a voice which was completely meaningless to him; after considerable persuasion I agreed to listen to it, fully convinced that he had imagined the whole thing. As far as I remember I must have listened to the section of the tape which had been pointed out to me for about ten minutes, and I was on the point of giving up when I suddenly noticed the peculiar rhythm mentioned by Raudive and his colleagues. After five or six more play-backs, out of the blue, I heard a voice. In my Preface to *Breakthrough* I have explained my reaction and the subsequent events.

This was the first of a great number of remarkable happenings which moved me to change my mind and recommend that Raudive's book should be published. In the following year I resigned my academic appointment and joined the publishing house of Colin Smythe as a full time director. Circumstances beyond my control made it necessary for me to involve myself more and more with the Voice Phenomenon until what had started as a publicity campaign for *Breakthrough* had turned into an independent investigation into the Phenomenon as such.

The publicity which was given to the Voices in the press, on radio and on television forced me to continue my investigation for many months after the publication of the Book. My aim in writing about the Phenomenon is to answer the most important question which I have been asked: "How dead are the voices?"

1

A Question of Belief

The question of life after death has occupied man's mind since first he became consciously aware of his existence. Every civilisation has evolved its own beliefs and ideas about the kind of post-mortal existence man would enjoy or suffer, once his physical activity on earth had come to an end. In many cases such an after-life was believed to be identical with the life man had lived on earth, with the same physical needs and desires. Other civilisations created a new dimension for their dead, an *Underworld*, a *Paradise* or a *Kingdom of Heaven*. Man's desire to communicate with the spirits of the dead goes back as far as his belief in an after-life.

There are three reasons why he wishes to speak to the dead or be spoken to by them: — 1) a personal and emotional reason, caused by the loss of a close friend or relation; 2) a sense of insecurity which moves him 'to seek guidance and oracles of ghosts and familiar spirits' (Isaiah), or in other words, to look upon death as the beginning of a more advanced and knowledgeable existence, in which the soul or spirit of the departed person gains advantages over man on earth, which he can share with the spirits through mediums, seers or other means of communication; 3) man's insatiable thirst for the truth: he reasons that death cannot be the end of his total existence and he therefore wants to gain material proof of survival. In this quest for the truth he tries to be objective and examines any evidence in the light of scientific probability. However, it is impossible for man to be completely unbiased and unprejudiced. He has a vested interest in the outcome of his investigation and research. Right from the start, he either seeks evidence of spiritual survival or proof that life after death is logically and scientifically impossible and only wishful thinking on the part of those who look for it. At the extreme ends of the scale we have, inevitably, those people to whom material evidence is a means to an end. To the vast majority of people material evidence either substantiates their religious beliefs or is in conflict with their philosophy of life. By the time we start thinking about life after death we are already pre-conditioned; our education, upbringing, religious or otherwise, political or economic environments, even the mood we are in when contemplating survival after death—all these factors determine not just our readiness to be objective in our evaluation of evidence, but our capacity to detach ourselves from human qualities which makes us a personality in contrast to a living computer. It may appear desirable to use a computer in evaluating such evidence; but we must recognise that a computer has to be fed its information by a person. It is therefore reasonable to assume that man's most advanced invention, the computer, will only yield the result we desire. The ultimate decision to accept or reject evidence of life after death can only rest with man. Of course, he can abdicate his right of decision making; a church, an organisation or even a political party may be entrusted by its members to make decisions by proxy. The physical power at the disposal of such a body corporate determines the degree of conformity within its ranks.

Most of us owe a degree of allegiance to a body corporate; all of us were, at one time or other, pre-conditioned to a philosophy of life. Whatever evidence is put before us, our initial reaction will be in line with pre-conceived ideas. Our second reaction will be to weigh information against other evidence or doctrines and to seek a basis on which to justify our reaction and subsequent standpoint in a logical manner; if we are still uncertain, we ask for more evidence and finally for the approval or disapproval of those whom we believe to be more qualified.

This is exactly what has happened since strange, unaccountable voices were recorded on a tape recorder by Friedrich Jürgenson in 1959. The 'electronic voices', as they came to be known, first of all presented a puzzle to electronics experts: as the number of recordings increased, so the puzzle became more difficult because not only were the voices impossible to explain from a scientific point of view, but the contents of speech, the communication of intelligible thought forms, presented additional problems. The first reaction, in accordance with our pre-conditioned reasoning, was to explain the voices as freak pick-ups or random radio waves. For about five years, scientists attempted to break this electronic mystery; it was then that a theory was put forward which is still under discussion today, that these voices must be of para-normal origin. The word para-normal simply means that something cannot be explained in normal physical terms. Normally there is no room for anything para-normal in applied science: if the voices do not originate from random but accountable radio waves, then the only possibility of determining their origin lies in excluding all radio waves from manifesting themselves on an electro-magnetic tape by a process of elimination. This science can do and has done, but the voices continue to manifest themselves. The only logical action left therefore, was to consider where such voices could originate. Three possible sources are: —

1) electronic impulses sent out by our subconscious mind and registered as human speech on the tape.

2) voices transmitted by an unknown method from perhaps another planet or an intelligent source somewhere in the universe.

3) people who have died on this earth and try to retain communication with those who are still here: in fact, that the voices originate from where they say they do.

Another explanation of the phenomenon, might be that these voices are not there at all and are just imagined. This explanation can now be discarded as wrong, since voice recordings have been printed on a visible speech printer, and can also be seen on oscillographs where they register as visible impulses, we can only accept the fact that they really are there.

This leaves 1) to 3) to choose from. The only evidence we can take into consideration and examine is the speech content. This then must be seen in relation to our understanding, logic, relevance and even the personal wishful thinking of the listener. On this basis of elimination, it soon becomes obvious that point 2) as a possible source of the voices can not apply. No indication or even suggestion is contained in the many thousands of voices recorded which could justify the theory that another planet or intelligent being from somewhere in the universe is attempting to get in touch with us.

The insignificance, even banality of much of the speech content points to a not entirely unfamiliar pattern of human thought-forms, namely what we experience in dreams. Professor Dr. Hans Bender of the University of Freiburg, Germany retains, however, such an explanation as a possible alternative. He asks the question whether it is not possible for the subconscious to send out impulses which register on the tape as a human voice. Bender's theory would, of course, be strengthened if the languages recorded by an experimenter were always those understood or spoken by himself or any one of the persons present during the experiment. For some time a number of case histories have been known where voices were recorded in a language which was neither spoker nor understood by the experimenter or his immediate circle of collaborators. Another factor to observe is that while the subconscious may well send out impulses, they would be unlikely to register as something so artificial as human speech. There is a substantial difference between a thought-form and its conversion into the spoken word. The latter is a conscious action which is often none too easy and can require a conscious effort.

The case histories of Dr. Raudive are not typical and

cannot really be taken as evidence for disproving Bender's theory because different languages are spoken in one sentence. Even the misuse of language and grammar in many of Raudive's recordings does not prove Bender wrong. On the contrary, the polyglot nature of Raudive's experiments is no handicap to his ability to understand them. His interpretation of speech content often differs greatly from that of other listeners, and recent examinations by David Ellis, who is studying the Voice Phenomenon under the auspices of Trinity College, Cambridge, have shown that Dr. Raudive has been known to interpret radio pick-ups as genuine Voice Phenomena. But as most of his case histories are examined independently, and many of his recordings are conducted by a group of scientists, such cases of misinterpretation are far and few between. But I have noticed myself that on occasions, perhaps because he is pressed too hard by observers, Konstantin Raudive is capable of making mistakes which could be used as evidence against him.

As I mentioned before, a number of experimenters have received voice recordings which could not be translated or interpreted by them or anybody connected with the experiment. These were later found to be in a foreign language but quite coherent in content. As the conditions under which the recordings were made exclude the possibility of freak pick-up from outside transmitters, Professor Bender's theory or alternative explanation cannot apply in such cases. Therefore the theory does not provide a scientifically valid solution, but this is not the only reason for refusing to accept the 'animistic' theory: the chances against a series of electronic impulses from the subconscious manifesting themselves in sounds which correspond—even remotely—to common speech in any language are mathematically so great and improbable that they must be ruled out. The proverbial chimpanzee at the piano has a far better mathematical chance of playing all of Beethoven's sonatas than a single thought form has of manifesting itself through electronic impulses and recording itself as human speech.

It is the third explanation that *Breakthough* and this book are concerned with. Having been unable to explain the Phenomenon with our pre-conceived ideas about its possible origin, and after tentative dismissal of points 1) and 2), we asked for more evidence to substantiate the case that these voices originated from those we knew had died. Throughout the process of examining the additional evidence we have sought approval from those whom we believed to be more qualified than we were, in order to come to a decision. The struggle for the truth, the disappointments and successes along the path of discovery are as important as the truth itself. All I endeavour to do here is to 'take stock' of what is there and what is missing. The German, Swedish and some other European scientists, philosophers and theologians have often been primarily concerned with discovering an *absolute* truth and with the presentation of final, unchangeable dogmas. In Britain and Ireland, those who have studied the Voice Phenomenon have been concerned with a *relative* truth and placed the human being with all his faults, shortcomings and emotions top of the list of priorities. In Germany, especially, scientists, psychologists and theologians have been digging their entrenched positions from which they fight each other's theories: once a position is taken up, that is the end of it. The guarding of personal reputation and position becomes ultimately far more important than the object of the exercise. 'Those who are not for me, are against me' is still very much the slogan of the intellectual leadership.

The arrival, development and public demonstration of the electronic Voice Phenomenon in the British press is worth while studying, quite apart from its validity as a para-normal or psychic phenomenon. This record will also help in establishing which questions have been asked and answered satisfactorily and which problems remain still to be solved; it may even help in preventing the time-consuming repetition of arguments, and give to those who are interested in the Voice Phenomenon a chance to carry on the discussion from where others have left off. Any criticism

I make in the course of this narrative is my own personal opinion which I do not expect to be shared by every reader. I have been far too involved in the whole matter to remain completely objective and unbiased, and the reader must bear this in mind when judging my personal evidence. Wherever I have quoted somebody else's opinion, I have done so verbatim and from authentic records.

2

Full of Surprises

During one of the television programmes on the electronic voices from the dead, the interviewer asked me whether I regretted having cast my vote in favour of Dr. Raudive's book *Breakthrough*, and whether I would do so again had I known in advance of the widspread controversy which would follow publication. After all, for seven months I was prevented from carrying out my normal work as a publisher; my entire energy and 16 hours out of every 24 had been taken up with acting as an unpaid PR man for the strangest and oddest clients that could be anybody's misfortune to represent: purported voices from the dead.

With only thirty seconds left to answer this last question of a half-hour interview, and having learned the importance of getting the last word in a programme like this, my main concern was naturally to prevent the interviewer or another panelist making a final remark which might have ruined the impression I had built up over the previous twenty nine minutes. Hence I explained that I had not regretted anything: on the contrary, I had enjoyed every moment, and I carried on talking until I saw the programme fading out on the little monitor in front of me.

Of course, the truth is that on occasions I have regretted the initial enthusiasm which prompted me to accept the promotion of *Breakthrough;* but the reasons for my regret have nothing to do with my belief that the Voice Phenomenon is genuine, though it is fair to say that there have been moments when I wished I had never heard of Raudive or the electronic voices!

Right from the start, back in 1969, when I met Konstantin Raudive for the first time, his attitude and mine to those voices were quite different. To Raudive these voices were as necessary as the air he breathed. He showed contempt for those who did not immediately agree with his theories and people who could not understand his highly intellectual and philosophical monologues did not interest him at all. Like a quiet, friendly gentleman who becomes an aggressive and quarrelsome driver as soon as he has taken his position behind a steering wheel, Dr. Raudive tends to take on a different personality behind the tape recorder and generally when discussing the electronic voices.

Let me make this clear right here and now, I believe *Breakthrough* to be a collection of important research material; I cannot think of another researcher whose single-mindedness of purpose has yielded such a wealth of information, and Raudive's work deserves due acknowledgement and the most serious consideration. On the other hand, his book is so involved and complicated that readers with little patience and people with no academic training find it heavy going. In my opinion, Raudive's theories are not the kind which are likely to convince an objective observer that the facts on which they are based are correct or that a breakthrough into another dimension has been achieved. The evidence from electronic experts and other scientific researchers is far more impressive; Raudive's work supplies excellent corroborative evidence, and as long as his theories of what he believes is happening do not overstep the factual evidence available, the mystery of the Voice Phenomenon can be explained and discussed within the framework of logic and reasoning. This has been my dilemma: I am about as qualified to talk about electronics as I am to talk about nuclear physics. All I have been interested in is the human aspect of this remarkable discovery. I believe that anything which might shed light on to the uncertainty of death, is as important to the most simple and ordinary person as it is to scientists, professors or eminent churchmen.

I have been asked many times whether I was afraid of death and if the voices had removed such a fear. The true answer to this is that I don't know. I have always looked upon death as a door. What I am probably afraid of is what happens before I pass through that door. The suffering, the loss of faculties and the awareness of breaking human relationships while awaiting death and the pain and agony which might precede it are what I fear. Like all people I have ever spoken to, I hope that death will come quickly and suddenly. I prefer not to know when it will happen. The voices make death no more palatable than it has been. Yet the prospects of life after death fascinate me; I do not fear the loss of material possessions nor the fact that my physical presence has come to an end. If I could be sure of a quick and sudden death, I would certainly answer that I am not afraid of it; it is the process of dying I don't look forward to. Besides, my only experience has been that of an observer; I have suffered the loss of people I loved, I have been the one who was left behind and had to cope with the material aspects and duties of the 'bereaved'. Therefore, anything that could comfort me in my wish to know that the departed were happy or content after passing through that door, is of great importance to me, knowing that sooner or later I have to pass through that same door myself.

In this sentiment I am not alone; it is shared with most people, irrespective of their intelligence, their academic qualifications or their position in life.

The question about who ought to be interested in the Voice Phenomenon has been one of the major points of difference between Dr. Raudive and myself. His extremely complicated and involved style of writing proved almost impossible to translate into the English language. Time and time again he refused to have sentences simplified because he felt that such editorial changes would lessen the impact of his theories. He was afraid of being made to look foolish in the eyes of scientists and of sounding too *ordinary* and *simple.*

After my resignation from academic teaching and becoming a full-time publisher, Raudive's *The Inaudible Becomes Audible* was the first project I was given to see through the stages of translation, editing and production. I had planned to get the book to the printers within five months; Nadia Fowler and Joyce Morton completed their task well within that time, but in Colin Smythe's opinion and my own it had become a task of *making the unreadable readable.*

Instead of the five months I had planned for the preparation of copy it took us a year and a half which was entirely due to demands by Raudive for further changes and in my opinion unjustifiable additions. I felt particularly annoyed at his demands and peremptory orders concerning our use of the English language, and between 1969 and 1971 Colin Smythe and I at times even considered whether it might not be better to abandon the whole publishing project.

It was only because, in my opinion, the research into the Voice Phenomenon was an important and worthwhile subject for publication that I decided to write a Preface to the book. In it I justified our decision to publish the work and gave the names of scientists who had been involved in the research and whose reputations were known to me personally. Dr. Raudive returned a proof of my Preface with all references to one of the professors crossed out because he felt that this gentleman featured too prominently in my account. The name of another professor, of whom I had never heard before, had been substituted.

Needless to say, I did not alter my Preface but I handed the entire project over to my partner to see it through the final stages of production.

Judging by the hundreds of column inches of reviews on the book, it appears that the majority of the reviewers only enjoyed reading the Preface and some of the contributions by scientists at the end of *Breakthrough.* This has put me in an embarrassing position and is partly the reason for my appearing on all those television and radio programmes. In June 1971 a syndicated article appeared in a number of newspapers and magazines; in it the writer asks: "Why did Dr. Raudive not appear personally on television—or for that matter restrict his communication with the press representatives to experiments only? Instead, Peter Bander, one of the publishers of the book who had also written the Preface to Dr. Raudive's work, was introduced as 'the obvious choice'. Of course, it was Peter Bander who made the Voice Phenomena palatable to the masses and who really 'sold' the book . . . Yet listening to Mr. Bander, I had the distinct feeling that he was no disciple of Raudive; in fact I recall several occasions when he strongly dissociated himself from the author whose book he was presenting."

There is a small mistake in this paragraph. Raudive did not restrict himself to experiments; we only wished he had and that he had talked less about some of his pet ideas. I must take personal responsibility for not always translating what he said; (he did, for instance, explain his contempt of "popular" papers to Alan Whittaker of the *News of the World* without realising that this paper is aptly described by that adjective). When Raudive talked about his research he was excellent, but his long-winded Teutonic elaborations would have provided marvellous copy for an astute journalist like Alan Whittaker. As it happened, he got only the translation of the actual comments on the voices and the answers to his questions. The result was a sound and factual article in his paper on the following Sunday. I dread to think what might have appeared otherwise—it would have been funny, but not for the publishers of *Breakthrough*.

The meetings between Dr. Raudive and representatives of the press are of considerable importance in a true assessment of the Voice Phenomenon and I shall deal with them separately.

In my Preface to *Breakthrough*, I quoted extensively from the explanations given to me and my friends by an electronics engineer, David Stanley. It was mainly because

I did not understand the technical explanations by eminent scientists such as Professor Alex Schneider that I had asked Mr. Stanley to explain them to us in simple terms. This applied especially to the different methods of recording which Dr. Raudive had employed during his experiments. During the following months, Mr. Stanley's explanations were frequently endorsed by leading scientists and experts in the field of electronics. I had the benefit of David Stanley's endless patience and admirable gift of drawing. Unfortunately, only a fraction of his explanations could be included in my Preface; I was constantly worried about duplicating what had already been said by other experts later on in the book.

Because my Preface contains technical explanations and instructions it has always been assumed that I could elaborate on them further and I have often found myself in the unenviable position of being asked further to simplify the recording technique for television audiences. On one occasion, at the B.B.C. studio in Langham Place, Gyles Brandreth asked me to describe in layman's language what a diode was.

Facing me behind a glass partition were the sound engineers, obivously enjoying my predicament. I turned the tables on them and asked whether it would not be far better if one of them were to cut himself into the conversation and give the explanation. "A diode is what we used to call a cat's whisker" was the answer from the engineer. I am sure, if I had said that, Gyles would have pursued his enquiry but, coming from the sound engineer, it seemed to satisfy him. Only after the programme did he ask me "What on earth is a cat's whisker?"

This incident taught me a lesson. From then on I made sure that I always had an expert with me on programmes, or at least some written explanation to the usual technical enquiries. My main problem has been to present the Voice Phenomenon in such a way that the evidence I produced was verifiable and backed the principle of Dr. Raudive's book. Soon I noticed that critics were willing to accept

Raudive's research findings, but not his personal interpretations. A typical case in question is his statement on page 143 in *Breakthrough*. Here Raudive describes something that has happened during some experiments. For no known reason a number of voices manifest themselves simultaneously; after a while one of these voices predominates. In certain of Raudive's experiments this voice appears to take charge of further communications; at least this is how I understand it from the voice samples he produces. In cases of such overcrowding of voices which I have noticed myself during other experiments, I thought that one particular voice could be understood while others are too faint, and I put the difficulty down to interference. However, Raudive draws the conclusion that there is a customs post, where entities have to obtain a passport or licence to communicate with us. Needless to say, this and some similar interpretations and descriptions by Dr. Raudive were used by critics to pour cold water on the whole question of the voice phenomena.

Ted Bonner (RTE) commented on similar scenes which are recorded in the book. He felt that many of Raudive's recordings express a strong parochial, if not chauvinistic, attitude prevailing among some of the voices. They appear to be fighting, at least verbally. "Here are the Germans"—or "here are the Latvians"—are sentences which occur time and time again.

The voices of the famous or infamous which Raudive purports to have recorded have presented me with more difficulties during the discussions. I cannot help feeling that name-dropping, a very human weakness, has either entered the celestial realms or is being projected into them by Raudive. In fairness to the author I must say that it has been pointed out to me on several occasions that it was not unreasonable for those voices to dominate, as the purported originators during their lifetime on earth were equally vociferous. The fighting among those who left this earth seems to be substantiated by the opinions held by many Spiritualists. Lord Dowding wrote about his experiences during and after the war when in 'rescue circles' many sincere and devout people helped those spirits to find tranquility and peace. Gordon Turner referred to his work in such rescue circles, and it is because of the nature of such recordings, that he believes it was wrong to have published those examples. The vast majority of the voices I have heard during the many tests and experiments carried out in my presence, seemed to come from persons who had a strong link with one or more of the experimenters. This can be explained far more easily than voices purporting to come from statesmen, famous authors and philosophers, with perhaps one notable exception, Carl Gustav Jung, the psychologist. His voice appears to manifest itself frequently during Raudive's recordings. Furthermore, what the voice purports to be saying makes sense. Another observation I have made is that all the voices we have received during a great number of experiments were attributable to persons who had died no longer than twenty or thirty years ago; also, when first manifesting themselves, they show definite characteristics of anxiety and eagerness.

Among Raudive's thousands of voice samples are some which deserve special mention; they are different from the others, not only in clarity but in speech content. The outstanding voice among those is that purporting to belong to Margarete Petrautski. It has been recorded in different countries without Raudive being actually there. She was a close friend of both Raudive and his wife, Dr. Zenta Maurina, and acted as secretary to them. Almost immediately after her death, a voice was recorded calling out "Zenta"—there followed the name "Margarete" and the remarkable statement "Bedenke ich bin" (German: "Imagine, I really exist," or "I really am"). I was so impressed by this voice that I first rejected the title *Breakthrough* for the book and suggested "Imagine, I Am", but I was persuaded that such a title would have been meaningless to anyone seeing the book and not knowing what it was all about.

Very much to my surprise, Mr. Michael Taunton, who has been conducting his own private experiments in East London, reports a series of voice recordings which point to originators whom he has never known; among them was a voice calling: "Margarete" and then "Raudive". A similar recording was made by Mr. Colin Smythe two years ago, before he even knew of Miss Petrautski's relationship to Dr. Raudive.

I have come to the conclusion that the stronger the affinity has been between two people during their lifetime, the greater the chance of a voice manifesting itself after one of them has died. I stress, however, that this is purely a casual observation I have made, and I cannot prove it with hard scientific facts.

No data or rules for recording conditions have been evolved so far. Dr. Raudive does not give details, for example, on weather conditions during his recordings, yet I am certain that atmospheric conditions are important. Several times experimenters have asked the 'voices' for suggestions in regard to better recordings. There are, I believe, three or four references which point to the moon. Leslie Hayward made one recording where a voice says in answer to his question what the best time would be for recording them: "When the sun goes down".

However, there appears to be little information forthcoming from the voices which would revolutionise the reception quality. Another observation I have made concerns the strange rhythm in which these voices seem to fit as in a pattern. Once a voice has manifested itself in a particular rhythm, this seems to be adopted by all the voices which follow for a period of about an hour; then, quite suddenly, the rhythm changes. I have rarely heard two different rhythms in one recording which has been made within one hour; again, I have no explanation to offer. We know that there is no need to create an 'atmosphere' by dimming the lights or forming a circle, but recordings made in the evenings usually yield results more quickly. All but two of the experiments I have participated in were conducted under semi-clinical conditions; we were completely detached from the proceedings and simply operated the tape recorders. The results were fair and the speech content of the recorded voices was in most cases relevant. On the other hand, Raudive always personalises his experiments. He takes it for granted that there are a number of entities which will record their voices. He starts every experiment by first using the microphone method and introducing those present; he asks any friends who wish to talk to do so and then switches over to the diode method for the actual recordings. I don't mind broadcasting on the radio because I know that there are some people at the other end listening; in fact, I always make a point of speaking to some of my friends who I know are listening. But, sitting in a room with a tape recorder going, I find it difficult to adopt a natural manner in asking anybody whom I cannot see to speak on the tape. Yet I have noticed that such a 'personal' method of approaching voice recording yields far better results. On her first recording, Mrs. Pan Collins of RTE spoke freely and naturally to those who wished to comunicate via the tape and invited voices to manifest themselves. Taking into consideration that she used a tiny cassette tape recorder, which runs on batteries, she had far more success than many scientists have had with elaborate equipment; besides, her voices were of a personal nature and could be linked to people whom she had known. The question of personal magnetism or even mediumship will be raised a few times later on; I really don't know whether these play a part during the recording of voices. However, it has become evident that the positive attitude a person shows during an experiment is important as it contributes to better results.

I said at the outset that *Breakthrough* is an important collection of research material. Apart from this, the book also contains many personal opinions held by the author. It was unfortunate that we did not edit the book further. Those reviewers who have been critical based their criticisms on the author's personal opinions which, I admit, appear sometimes to be far fetched and illogical. Before the second *Late Late Show* on Telefis Eireann, Ted Bonner, an electronics expert with Decca, suggested that Raudive laid himself wide open to debunking. I retorted that nobody could debunk him better than I could, "but", I added, "that would be dishonest and unfair because the research speaks for itself; you cannot debunk the evidence, only the occasional comment." Ted Bonner agreed but warned me to be prepared for such attacks on Raudive's opinions, and of the danger that much time might be taken up with caustic comments, thus leaving little time to discuss the Voice Phenomenon as such. I owe much of the success of the many television programmes which followed to the sound advice of Ted Bonner. By stating at the beginning of each programme that I had not come to discuss Raudive's personal opinions and then concentrating on the subject matter rather than on the author, I have been able to explain more and create a bigger interest than might have been possible otherwise.

After I had read Raudive's German version of the book in 1969, I wrote down six questions:

1) Are there voices on the tapes which should not be there?
2) Can these voices be explained either electronically or psychologically?
3) Whose voices are they?
4) What do they say?
5) Has what they say any value?
6) Can anybody get these voices and hear them?

I scribbled my answers behind them.

1) Yes!
2) Not so far; electronic freak? Psychologically, no; Bender's alternative theory not viable.
3) They give names, but should we believe them?
4) On the whole nothing startling, although relevance and meaningfulness depend on interpretation by experimenter.
5) I don't know yet.
6) Theoretically, yes. In practice about 6 out of 10; will probably improve with better equipment.

It is difficult to improve on or add to the answers, but I can qualify them better. On the other hand, today I have many more questions and I am not sure that I could put even tentative answers behind them.

Victor Bearman wrote an article in the magazine *Light* and called it 'Full of Surprises'. He says that we always accept that life is full of surprises, but in his opinion, having studied the Voice Phenomenon, he now believes that there were probably far more surprises in death.

If Mr. Bearman is right—and he well may be—then we are in for some real surprises after we die. If Raudive's *research* is correct, then it looks as if life after death could be rather hectic, but were his personal *conclusions* accurate, death would lead us to some celestial madhouse.

c

3

Pride and Prejudice

I don't want to repeat myself and write the Preface to *Breakthrough* all over again. May it suffice to say that my first reaction to Raudive's German book was negative. However, two people who appeared in the book as collaborators of the author were Professor Gebhard Frei, D.D., Ph.D., and Professor Bender, Ph.D. Both gentlemen were known to me: Bender is a psychologist of international repute, and Frei an eminent theologian and psychologist, co-founder of the Jung Institute in Zurich, President of various learned societies and a most prolific writer with some 450 publications to his name.

There was just one snag: Professor Frei had died a few months before I read his contribution to Raudive's book. After I had satisfied myself that the contribution was genuine, I had to find out what the reaction of Professor Frei's Church was after the publication of his article. After all, he had been a Roman Catholic priest who belonged to the Mission Society of Bethlehem, and the President of the International Society of Catholic Parapsychologists. From personal experience on previous occasions I knew that the Church could invalidate the contribution if a statement was made to the effect that Frei's article had been written by a sick man, or that Professor Frei did not command the Church's authority to write such an article.

I took advantage of my friendship with the Apostolic Nuncio to Belgium, Luxembourg and the E.E.C., Archbishop H. E. Cardinale, and during one of my visits to him in Brussels, I explained my predicament. I also said that I would accept any information I might receive as a guide whether to put Professor Frei's article into the book or not, but also made it clear that a very negative report could mean that we would not publish at all. We were a relatively young publishing house, and the goodwill of all the Churches had been of material help with our first publications. (At a later date we handed a proof copy of the book to the Bishop of London to find out whether the Anglican Church would object to the contents.)

Archbishop Cardinale promised to investigate and let me have a comment one way or the other. In three weeks I had the report. It testified to the high integrity of the late Reverend Frei and showed that, until his death, his service to the Church and his judgements on parapsychological questions were held in the highest esteem.

With this information in hand, I proceeded to invite Dr. Raudive to come to England for his first demonstration. I have described this visit in part in the Preface to Raudive's book. Certain things happened that night which have had a profound effect on me but at the time I was unable to publish these facts.

Nine months later, when an Austrian newspaper published an inaccurate account of the demonstration, and because of an indiscretion on Raudive's part, the editor of *Psychic News* in London approached me and asked for the correct story, as it had been leaked already. They agreed, however, to change the names and references, so that the person in question was protected from unwanted publicity. I am now in a position to give the whole story. Among the guests I had invited for Saturday 13th December 1969, was the Right Reverend Monsignor Stephen O'Connor, V.G., Principal Roman Catholic Chaplain to the Royal Navy. As he came directly from an official function, he was still wearing his frockcoat. Dr. Raudive's English is somewhat limited, and he must have been under the impression that Mgr. O'Connor was the Bishop of London. In his correspondence

Raudive always referred to him as the Bishop of London. Hence I knew that the Austrian journalist could not have invented the story when he wrote in his article in June 1970 that Dr. Raudive had a remarkable session with the Catholic Bishop of London during which the Bishop's deceased friend had made contact with him.

However, this is what really happened. Mgr. O'Connor was completely hostile to the idea of communication with the dead, either by electronic means, or any other means, for that matter. Some of my friends teased him about his stubborn attitude. He absolutely refused to believe Raudive or the physicists, and generally mistrusted everybody in the room. In the end he asked for what appeared to all of us to be a miracle. He told Dr. Raudive he wanted somebody to speak to him personally, give his name, address him by name and tell him exactly where he was and then confirm whether these experiments were really true. "Only then will I be able to judge the validity of these experiments", he said.

The recording was made with a diode. In view of the late hour and because my guest wanted to leave, we did not check this particular tape until the next morning, and unless my own study was broken into during the few remaining hours of the night and somebody took the trouble of substituting another tape, identical in every respect but with a faked recording on it, I must accept that the recording we monitored the next morning was a genuine Voice Phenomenon. Perhaps I had better mention here that my Great Dane, Rufus, does not normally allow anybody to remove as much as a piece of paper from my study, and as he has taken to sleeping outside the study and adjoining bedroom door, I would vouch for the fact that the tape we monitored a few hours after the recording was the same one.

I cannot pretend that I understood a single word on the recording, but I could hear a voice; it was of modest quality. Raudive told us it was Russian; translated the voice said:

"Stefan is here.

But you are Stefan.

You do not believe me,
It is not very difficult, we will teach Petrus"
I kept the original tape and had a copy made for Dr. Raudive. I did not tell Monsignor O'Connor of the recording. About a year later, during an experiment at which Mr. Andy Wiseman of the BBC *Tomorrow's World* programme was present with two colleagues and Graham Rose of *The Sunday Times,* I remembered this particular tape. Mr. Wiseman is fluent in Russian and German; we played this tape a few times and Mr. Wiseman confirmed that the above sentences were actually on that tape. Naturally, he had not been present at the time of recording, nor did he know the circumstances under which the recording had been made. I then telephoned Mgr. O'Connor and invited him to come the next day. Steve O'Connor accepted my word about the content of the message. He explained to me that some years before he had been Senior Roman Catholic Naval Chaplain in Malta. A young naval subaltern of Russian descent was in the military hospital with a serious neurotic complaint. Although not a Catholic, the young man by the name of Stefan (Russian for Stephen) was helped by Fr. O'Connor, who also assured the young lieutenant that he could always call on him when in need. About three months later, Fr. O'Connor returned one night from a day's visitation and found the CID waiting for him. Some twenty witnesses had already made statements to the police that a young officer had been enquiring everywhere after him. Two hours before the priest's return home, the young lieutenant had committed suicide. Since then Monsignor O'Connor has always wondered whether he could have saved the boy's life if only he had returned earlier. However, this is an academic question. The fact remains that a voice came through in Russian (a language which the Monsignor did not understand), identified itself as Stefan, referred to him by his Christian name, told him that he did not believe and promised to teach Petrus (an obvious reference to the Holy See).

Mgr. O'Connor told me that on his retirement from the

Royal Navy I could reveal his identity. However, on Tuesday 19th October 1971, the day after he had returned from a holiday in the U.S.A., his housekeeper found him dead in bed. He had suffered a heart attack and died, aged 51. On 6th October he had sent me a card from New York. The message is short but relevant: *You must come here and talk about Breakthrough.* In a manner of speaking, Mgr. O'Connor has retired from the Navy, so I am now in a position to reveal his name: his position as a senior officer in the Royal Navy and a Papal Prelate made this impossible during his tenure of office.

This particular experiment had a profound influence on my attitude to the Voice Phenomena, even more than my first encounter with an electronic voice which I, rather reluctantly, accepted to be that of my mother*. Another incident, which also impressed me very much, took place on Sunday 4th January 1970. It differs from all previous and subsequent experiments in that I personally attempted to establish a dialogue with my parents.

Throughout all the experiments in which I have participated or which I have watched, I have been very self-conscious and, to a degree, embarrassed, because I have always found it very difficult to accept electronic communication with the dead as a matter of fact. On that Sunday evening, however, I was tired and exhausted from trying to come to a decision on an important and far-reaching issue. Another person's livelihood was at stake, and since Saturday morning I had been discussing the matter with my partner, Colin Smythe. On Sunday night I remember saying to Colin: "If these voices really work and if my parents are really here, then they must know how difficult it is for me to make up my mind. I may as well ask them,"—or words to that effect. I freely admit that this kind of indecision is very unlike me, but I have explained already that I was very tired. As a psychologist I tend to analyse behaviour,

*See Preface to *Breakthrough*

especially my own, and I detect an interesting aspect in what I actually said during the recording: "I will give father ten seconds, and mother twenty seconds to answer my questioning because my mother would anyhow talk more."—I then addressed myself to my father and said: "Father can you help me?" (in English). I waited ten seconds and then I said: "Mother, you know what I have to do, am I right in doing it?" I waited twenty five seconds and then switched the recorder off. I had used a diode (the same one which David Stanley had made up for me on the occasion of Dr. Raudive's visit in December). On playback, watching the revolution counter on the tape recorder, I heard within a fraction of the first revolution a man's voice. After only three playbacks, the contents were quite clear to me. The language used was a dialect in which my father used to speak to his intimate friends, (and although neither my mother nor I ever spoke it ourselves, we understood it): "Jung, wenn ich doch nur kuennt", (meaning: "Boy, if only I could"). The interesting word is "Jung". This was indeed the way my father used to address me when he was alive.

Then came the turn of my mother's answer; again within a fraction of a second after asking my question the answer had manifested itself. "Und trotzdem sagst Du nein."—A literal translation would mean "And you still say no."—However, seen in context and knowing my mother's way of speaking, I prefer to translate it: "Whatever I say, you still will do the opposite."

Although I have mentioned this incident to some friends, I have never written about it. Victor Bearman, some months ago, asked me for permission to quote part of the incident to discuss Professor Bender's theory that we may be picking up subconscious thought-forms.

The first electronic voice I ever heard, purporting to be my mother, and the two sentences above, are the only examples I can quote of a personal communication received.

With one exception, I have never again attempted to establish contact with any particular person. I shall give my reasons for that later; but basically, it was because I felt no need to do so.

The one exception caused a somewhat funny incident. Not that it was funny at the time; I frankly admit that I was startled, but only for about ten minutes. I am quite prepared to put the whole thing down to some strange coincidence. As a matter of fact, although no explanation or reason was ever offered by the electronics experts, I am sure, or almost sure, that we must have done something stupid and perhaps over-loaded the machine. I don't know, but I am not prepared to accept the incident as proof of anything! It would be far too embarrassing if I did! On that occasion in February 1971 a small group of researchers were in Colin Smythe's study. We had been discussing the poor quality of voices received, and I suggested the reason might be that Dr. Raudive always approached an experiment in a matter of fact way. He appeared to take it for granted that certain people ('on the other side') were there waiting for him to establish communication. We, on the other hand, tried to be very 'scientific'; I don't think any of us ever expected a voice to manifest itself. We lacked confidence, to say the least. The persons present that evening were Colin Smythe, Leslie Hayward, an assistant in the publishing house, David Stanley, an electronics engineer, David Ellis, a graduate from Cambridge who had recently received the Perrott-Warrick Studentship to investigate the Voice Phenomena, and myself. We decided to reconstruct the type of recording session we had seen conducted by Raudive. I offered to take the chair and do the talking. The tape recorder used was a Bang & Olufsen, Beocord 2000, a rather elaborate and fairly expensive instrument. We started with a microphone recording, as Raudive always did. I gave the names of those present and asked anybody who wished to get in touch with us to speak as soon as we had switched over to the diode. The first experiment lasted three minutes and did not yield a single sound. "Perhaps we have done it wrong again", I suggested, "I am going for a certainty now. I shall ask my mother to speak; I am going even further than that. There is one temptation my mother could not resist, and that is the chance of stopping me smoking. She tried very hard during her life-time, and I am now prepared to give it up immediately, if she tells me to do so. All I want my mother to do is to say 'stop smoking' or anything to that effect. But it must be clear for everybody to hear." We started the recording again; this time I addressed my mother, inviting here to speak and offering, as a kind of bargain, to give up smoking. We had agreed to run this recording for three minutes. After two minutes were up, I remember saying: "Mother, if you want to speak and you have not done so, you have exactly thirty seconds in which to do so." I also remember making a joke about her not being able to resist such a golden opportunity. What happened then is difficult to explain. I had hardly finished my sentence when dark grey smoke started to pour out of the tape recorder, and I don't mean something like cigarette smoke; this dark smoke oozed out of every opening, at the controls, the buttons and through the ventilator holes. For a moment we were so surprised that nobody had the presence of mind to get up and pull the lead out of the socket. Of course, the shock only lasted two or three seconds, but the result was a ruined tape recorder; it took three months for it to be repaired at considerable cost to the owner. I still don't know whether I should have offered to pay at least half the bill because I don't know whether I am responsible. But, joking aside, the incident is certainly curious. There was no voice on the tape; after careful consideration (which took about one hour, during which I did not light a cigarette), I came to the conclusion that I had only offered to stop smoking if a voice actually said so. I beg the reader not to take this incident too seriously: it is interesting, even fascinating, but I hope that I don't get hundreds of letters telling me that I should have stopped smoking. I can think of some very sound reasons for giving it up, and I am actually considering those at the moment.

Psychologically, and especially from a parapsychological point of view, this experiment contains some worth-while aspects; unfortunately, we did not know in advance what was going to happen, or we might have invited psychic researchers to be present, but they might have said I had booby-trapped the machine. Afterwards I made everybody present promise not to talk about it. They all kept their promise. I certainly did not want to tell the story; all I was looking for was confirmation from others that the whole thing was a coincidence. I also believe that this incident and my reaction to it have proved that my personal attitude to such penomena is exceedingly sceptical. I think if I had heard a voice say on the tape "Give up smoking immediately", I would have been deeply shocked. This may sound illogical and I am prepared to be criticised. I just cannot jump over my own shadow. An explanation could possibly be found on the lines of "doctor, heal thyself"; as long as those messages are for others I think I can remain reasonably objective. It is the personal and emotional aspect of those voices (or of any phenomenon) that I find difficult to accept; perhaps I never believed that it could happen to me.

The months between Raudive's first visit in December 1969 and his second visit, one week before publication date (22—27 March 1971) were very hectic. The production of the book was delayed, and although we originally intended to publish in November 1970, in June we realised that this would be quite impossible.

Dr. Raudive's demands and complaints about the translation and editing arrived twice weekly, and we often discussed the advisability of abandoning the whole book. It seemed to make little difference to Raudive that I also speak German fluently and was therefore in a position to offer advice or constructive criticism. I remember one passage of six whole pages which I simply could not understand, let alone translate; Nadia Fowler found it impossible to put them into English. We therefore had a meeting with the Secretary of the Churches' Fellowship for Psychical Research, Victor Bearman, who after long deliberations suggested that those pages had better not be included in the translation. However, Joyce Morton made one last attempt to condense in one small paragraph the general idea expressed in those pages. We sent this to Raudive for his consent.

In his opinion our effort deserved no serious consideration; he felt that his *unique work* had been treated in an incompetent and ludicrous manner, and that his words could never be edited or translated into a simpler form. Such complicated and entirely new *thought forms* as he had used in his German book could never be rendered in sentences which could be easily understood. Raudive informed us that he would not tolerate any changes whatever and that he looked upon our efforts as *a betrayal of the truth*.

My own advice and criticism were dismissed because he felt that I obviously approved of such nonsense as our editor had written, and he rejected criticism from those whom we had mentioned because he thought it an impertinence for ignorant people, whom he considered of no importance, to criticise him. Throughout his complaints he made it clear that he looked upon our suggestions and comments from British parapsychologists which we had sent to him, as a *stylistic massacre* of his work.

By summer 1970 I made the decision to change publication date for *Breakthrough* from November to February '71, a date which we had to change yet again because of the postal strike. The foremost problem was, however, how we could present the Voice Phenomenon to the English speaking world without the full co-operation of the author in case he refused to take our advice in regard to the British press. Another point was also worrying me: during Raudive's first visit to England in 1969, Gerd Lüdemann of the German Press Agency and a prominent parapsychologist had introduced him to two well-known electronics experts of Belling and Lee Ltd. We were looking forward to their assistance and support in getting the Voice Phenomenon independently investigated in Britain and counted on their willingness to organise controlled tests. No sooner had Raudive returned to Germany than he informed us that the questions and problems which had been raised by the British electronics experts were *far too elementary* for his taste and that he was quite satisfied with the help he got from German experts. Whilst I have always considered myself to be in a privileged position with regard to Raudive and therefore unable to publish his letters, it is important that I explain the differences of opinion which have existed between us almost right from the start.

I was in the unenviable position of being his publisher after having suggested the publication of his work when my academic and personal opinion was sought by the publishing house in the first instance. To my mind it was only possible to present this remarkable discovery to the general public with the help and co-operation of British experts; if Raudive were to consider their methods of investigation unacceptable he would altomatically jeopardise the success of his book and land us with great financial losses.

As a trained psychologist I strongly challenge some of his theories and as his publisher I give reasons why we did not shorten the book and edit it more drastically. The press has widely criticised us for presenting long and indigestible passages of weird philosophy; Dr. Raudive has publicly criticised us for having cut some of his passages out without his permission. It appears therefore that our good intentions have won us few friends. Be this as it may, my main concern is the truth about the Voice Phenomenon. When newspaper men wrote to me that I appeared to dissociate myself from Raudive's theories and that I was no disciple of his, they were right. However, I did not realise at the time that it was so obvious. I am particularly happy that the two electronics experts from Belling and Lee Ltd. have never ceased to give us their support; their contribution has been far from elementary.

In the summer of 1970 I received yet another blow; this time from an unexpected quarter. Our own Chairman, Sir Robert Mayer, threw a spanner in the works. In mid-summer Colin Smythe had gone to Dublin on business. There he met Mr. Erskine Childers, the Deputy Prime Minister. Over lunch he told Mr. Childers of this remarkable book which we were to bring out in November. Mr. Childers, a close friend of our Chairman, wrote to Sir Robert, who was on holiday in Italy, and mentioned the possible repercussions such a publication could have if it did not get the backing of British scientists. Of course, he was absolutely right, and Sir Robert despatched a memorandum to me by express, laying down conditions on which he would insist if he were to give his blessing to the publication. A series of controlled experiments were to be arranged in the presence of independent experts. However, he was prepared to leave the general policy in this matter entirely in my hands as long as I promised not to compromise the publishing house with a publication which would be scoffed at by every electronics expert in the country.

With the assistance of some friends we set up our own recording equipment and tried to get voices, so that we could demonstrate to Sir Robert, on his return, the validity of Raudive's claim. At the time it looked hopeless to count on Raudive's personal support for any demonstration under controlled conditions. I suggested in a letter to him that he ought to agree to a demonstration on television. He liked the idea but laid down his own terms. During a telephone conversation he outlined what he thought ought to happen on British television: he would bring some of his tapes and first give a lecture, lasting about an hour; this would be followed by the playing of voice examples from his archives. When I told him that this was out of the question and explained that other scientists would have to do the experimenting and supervision of new experiments, he wrote back: "This subject matter is, as I have said before, a new one, and I am afraid that apart from myself nobody will be able to understand its intricacies, not even the most experienced parapsychologists."

Our own experiments were not paritcularly successful. We used only the diode and microphone methods and received far fewer and less audible voices than we had heard produced by Raudive. Although I was personally satisfied that the voices existed, I now realised the limitations in producing them. My hopes of recording something sufficiently impressive that could stand up to investigation, independently of Raudive, faded rather quickly. Our voices could not stand comparison with those on Raudive's tapes.

During September 1970, I had reached the point where just one more blow might have caused me to call the publication off. The two people who had never doubted for a moment that the project should be seen through, were Colin Smythe and Leslie Hayward. They turned up one morning with a cutting from a newspaper which said that the Perrott-Warrick post-graduate Studentship for Psychic Research, which is administered by Trinity College, Cambridge, had been awarded to David Ellis, M.A., for the investigation of the "Raudive Voices". To me this was the most welcome news; between now and publication date sufficient evidence might become available to demonstrate the Phenomenon publicly.

A second, though slightly more obscure, incident had also given me new hope. In a prominent article in the German newspaper *Das Bild Am Sonntag* (The Sunday Picture), mention was made of an electronics engineer from Cologne who had been engaged by the editor to attend a demonstration at Raudive's home in Bad Krozingen. From the article I gathered that this engineer was fully convinced of the genuineness of the Phenomenon. I telephoned the paper and found out the engineer's name: Hans Schauff. My attempts to reach him through the international directory service of the Post Office failed. However, my cousin, Mrs. G. Bienzeisler, whose offices are in Cologne, found him for me. Her enquiry whether he was willing to collaborate with a firm of British publishers on Raudive's book was met with a firm "no", but he offered to write his own story if we made him a tempting offer. "Once bitten, twice shy"; I was in no mood to make any more offers, but I was now certain that if a German electronics engineer after only one experiment could write a story, I did not have to worry about British engineers altogether failing to carry out successful experiments.

In December 1970, I established contact with David Ellis. We met and discussed in general terms what might be done in order to produce some viable results. I also wrote a brief synopsis of the book as it would appear in February and gave it to two experienced journalists to read, Miss P. M. Thompson of *The Bookseller* and Fred Salfeld, the editor of the Peterborough column in *The Daily Telegraph*. Their reaction, quite independently arrived at, was the same: "This is fantastic and tremendously interesting; it will certainly cause a controversy, but you must be able to prove the Phenomenon. Unless you can get Raudive over here to demonstrate before the press, or get somebody else to do so, nobody will take this seriously." Of course, that was what I had expected. Fred Salfeld retired from his editorial position at the end of 1970 and on 29th December he telephoned me and asked whether I was willing to let him do a piece on the voices and the forthcoming book in his last column. I agreed, although I had decided not to publicise the book until the last moment. On 30th December, Peterborough's last column finished with:

ELECTRONIC GHOSTS

A storm-raising book is every publisher's dream and it may be realised in March when Colin Smythe issue Konstantin Raudive's "Breakthrough", which makes the extraordinary claim that the voices of the dead can be recorded on tape.

Dr. Raudive, a German psychologist, apparently met, while recording bird songs,* a phenomenon predicted over 30 years ago by Sir Oliver Lodge. The idea of electronic communication with another world seemed fantastic, but it is now supported by respectable German, French and Italian scientists and thelogians and 25,000 examples have been recorded.

Colin Smythe invited Dr. Raudive to give a demonstration in London exactly a year ago and it now remains

*This was unfortunately inaccurate.

43

for his conclusions to be examined. They are being taken so seriously in Cambridge that Trinity College has given a scholarship for the investigation of them. Moreover, it seems that any reader of "Breakthrough" will be able to share in the experiment and draw his own conclusions.

As a result, we received many enquiries from other newspapers and television producers. I resisted the temptation of getting publicity for the book because I was unable to back Raudive's theories and claims with independent evidence. David Ellis, on the other hand, had accepted an invitation from Anglia Television, but in the words of one of the producers, "it was the biggest non-event in the whole programme." In my opinion, this had nothing to do with Ellis; he just could not tell the interviewer very much. He had met Raudive only once, during the *Imago Mundi* Conference, and not participated in an actual experiment. (Five months later I spoke to the same producer when we discussed another programme; he told me that at the time of the first interview he had been convinced that the Voice Phenomenon was just a joke.)

In January 1971 the publication date had to be postponed again. The Post Office strike caused chaos; no more proofs were received from the printers, some completed sections had not been delivered by the time the strike started and had to be printed again. A day or so before the strike started, a parcel purporting to contain a large section of proofs arrived empty, and we had to get the galley sheets from Slough, Maidenhead and other sorting offices where they had found their way. In addition, hundreds of letters and leaflets which we had promised for the book trade could not be sent out.

As much of a publisher's business is done by post, the strike provided us with more time to pursue an intensive research into the voices. David Stanley, the electronics enginneer whom I had consulted a year before, agreed to participate in a series of experiments, and David Ellis joined us for some evenings. The sessions lasted usually from seven in the evening until the early hours of the morning. From time to time I received a request from Sir Robert Mayer to be present at these experiments but I always managed to find an excuse to put him off. I knew Sir Robert well enough not to present anything to him that did not come up to his standard of perfection. Patience is a luxury Sir Robert does not indulge in, and the months of January and February would have tempted the patience of saints.

4

Trial and Error

The purpose of our investigation was to find the answers to many questions; I have already mentioned that Raudive's voices were of a better quality. They appeared to need fewer playbacks in order to understand them. On the other hand, Dr. Raudive's interpretations seemed to prejudice our own opinion, and often we disagreed strongly with him over what we understood the voices to have said. Furthermore, much of Raudive's output seemed to be in Latvian, a language none of us understood. (In fact, a large majority of the sentences recorded by him have been classified as being in Latvian.) The problem of interpreting voices turned out to be one of the most difficult handicaps we encountered from then on.

Another point, which later on became the main target for critics, especially on television, was the irrelevant content of the sentences recorded. Naturally, this problem is closely linked with the interpretation in the first place. I soon discovered that the messages which were clearly understood by the experimenters were meaningful in content as well. But such messages were far and few between. Nevertheless, Raudive had already collected some 72,000 different voices, and he quoted many thousands of these in the book. The voice examples which had been sent to us (about 300) had already Raudive's translation and interpretation on the tape; he also explained in detail the significance or relevance of these voices. However, none of these could be admitted as evidence and I was far from being satisfied that they were really relevant. After all, if something is to be meaningful, it has to be relevant, either to me personally or to a situation in which I am involved. During the next two months we encountered perhaps five such voices, but then we did not go in for quantity but quality.

We arranged our first meeting on 21st January, 1971 and a number of interested parties met in Gerrards Cross. Among them, Colin Smythe, David Ellis, Ralph Lovelock, a physicist and electronics engineer from Belling and Lee Ltd., David Stanley, Gerd Lüdemann, a parapsychologist and correspondent of the German Press Agency, who had followed Raudive's progress over a number of years, Victor Bearman, Gyles Brandreth, of the BBC and also a director of Colin Smythe Ltd., Nadia Fowler, Leslie Hayward and some other members of our publishing house.

Most of us had, at one time or other, seen Raudive at work or at least discussed the Voice Phenomenon with him. Early on in the evening David Ellis gave a report of his research so far. Of particular interest was his account of the *Imago Mundi* Conference in Austria which had taken place between 17th and 20th September 1970 and which Ellis had attended as an observer. The theme of the Conference had been "The World, Man and Tomorrow's Science", an appropriate platform for Dr. Raudive to present his research. The convening body of this Conference is the International Society for Catholic Parapsychologists. Papers are read by the leading Catholic scientists on questions concerning social problems, psychology, parapsychology and modern physics and, on this occasion, an entire afternoon was given to four papers read by Dr. Raudive, Theodor Rudolph, a high frequency engineer with Telefunken, Germany, Professor Alex Schneider, a physicist from Switzerland, and Franz Seidl, an electronics engineer from Austria. During his stay on the Continent, Mr. Ellis had visited a number of scientists, but his actual experience of the Voice Phenomenon was limited to listening to tapes which had already been recorded. Mr. Ellis explained to us his uneasiness about Dr.

Raudive's interpretations of many voices and said that in the opinion of some Continental scientists it would take up to ten years before a more reliable and qualitatively better recording apparatus could be perfected. We also heard of Mr. Rudolph's *Gonimeter* and Mr. Seidl's *Psychofon,* two rather more sophisticated recording mechanisms which may or may not provide the first step towards a more reliable method of recording voices.

After the general discussion we decided to carry out a few experiments of our own. For these we used two tape recorders, a Bang & Olufsen Beocord 2000, and a Ferguson 4-track mono recorder. David Stanley had built a bank of inputs for ear phones so that four people could listen to the playback simultaneously. Ellis had brought a stereo amplifier whic he used for a separate set of ear phones; for our recordings we chose the diode method. We made several recordings, each lasting between two and three minutes; most of the time was spent on 'playback'. All of those present, with the exception of David Ellis, heard voices; however, only one of them, recorded on the Ferguson, was clear enough to be understood without difficulty. A voice said "Mutter" (German: 'Mother'). I don't think we looked upon our experiments as a brilliant success. One point in particular had caused great inconvenience, the time-consuming playbacks. Often, after hearing the rhythm of a voice, we lost it when we moved the tape back to repeat the playback.

Between the first session and the next, on January 26th, I gave some thought to this problem, and it occurred to me that a solution might be found in using tape loops. Colin Smythe and I cut up a spool of recording tape and made a number of 32in. loops, which would play back any message every $8\frac{1}{2}$ seconds. As a first step, we made loops from previous recordings, among them the first voice I had ever heard, some 14 months earlier. I noticed with some relief that even Ellis heard this particular voice. That night we made two new recordings. This time, the tables were turned; I appeared to be the only one who did not hear anything while the others were quite excited about both loops. This may have been due to some facts which I have verified on later occasions. Normally, we would always switch the telephone bells off, i.e. the four telephones on the first floor, if we experimented in either Colin Smythe's or my study. I would also use a set of earphones and listen to some earlier recordings to acclimatise my hearing to the peculiar frequency and rhythm. After about ten minutes, I usually felt I would be able to hear any unusual manifestations on new recordings. During the evening of the 26th, I had to make a number of telephone calls and also spent some time in a room where the telephones were ringing frequently. Later I realised that nothing impedes one's hearing more than the piercing noise of a telephone bell, but that night I paid no particular attention to this fact and went back to the study where the experiments were carried ou. For about half an hour, I heard absolutely nothing, just the hissing and "white" noise on the tape. I was almost on the verge of calling it a day when I noticed a rhythm; within a minute I distinctly heard the word 'David'. Earlier on, we had agreed not to tell each other what we would hear but write it down next to the number shown on the revolution counter. When we compared notes, Ellis had put down 'Raudiv', Smythe had put down 'Raudive', Hayward, 'David' and I had put down 'David' as well. I was quite sure that 'David' was right and not 'Raudive' or 'Raudiv'. I insisted on doing yet another recording, and I told Leslie Hayward quietly that I would mentally ask for confirmation, expecting to get 'David' yet once again. I immediately heard the three syllables and vowels 'o', 'e' and 'i'; after five more playbacks the consonants then fell into place: 'John Ellis'. Hayward and Smythe heard it, but they might well have been influenced by me; we tried another twenty or thirty times, always coming back to 'John Ellis'. It was then that David Ellis told us of his second Christian name: John. All I can say is that if the recording we made really says 'John Ellis', it certainly would provide a remarkable confirmation of the first recording we had done. However, the voice was

49

too faint for amplification or to be used for a demonstration. While our mental attitude was prejudiced at that time, nevertheless this type of relevant recording was exactly what we were looking for.

Some very interesting experiments took place on 29th January. David Stanley and Ellis had suggested four different experiments. 1) With a diode, 2) with no input at all, 3) with a noise generator, and 4) with a diode on an extended lead of approximately 10 feet between the tape recorder and the diode. Again we used tape loops. The voices we recorded were, although faint, quite clear and, what was most important, relevant to the proceedings.

When we used the noise generator, we received a voice saying: "This noise—is no good". When using the long lead on the diode, a voice said: "Cut the wire". But David Ellis began to be weary of the poor quality of voices received: obviously he had hoped for far better results after three experiments, especially as Raudive's voices, which he had listened to and amplified, were so much clearer. I admit to considerable impatience with Ellis at the time; in my opinion, research should always be accompanied by a positive attitude and the willingness to do better next time and not a negative attitude of holding long inquests on something that has failed. It also became clear that David Ellis meant to 'sit on the fence' at any price. His supervisor, appointed by the awarding board of the Studentship, was Mr. J. H. Cutten, the Secretary of the Society for Psychical Research. Some members of the S.P.R. had informed me that the opinion of the S.P.R. was divided on the subject of the Voice Phenomenon. Mr. Cutten belongs to the more vociferous group which had already made up their minds that the origin of the voices was to be found anywhere but not in the psychic field. Some believed that these voices might come from Flying Saucers.

Mr. Ellis' dependence on Mr. Cutten's opinion is revealed in his second preliminary report (published 2nd February 1971) in which he states: "My Supervisor, Mr. Cutten, suggested that if I adopt at different times the viewpoints of the Spiritualists and of the sceptic who rejects Spiritualism, I would be less likely to miss possible alternative explanations."

This is exactly what David Ellis has done. Mr. Cutten's advice was, in my opinion, wrong; I speak with some experience, because I have spent six years as a tutor advising students on research methods. In my opinion, it would have been far better not to have included Spiritualism in the terms of reference because Ellis was supposed to examine and investigate a scientific phenomenon. Dr. Raudive has put forward a theory of post-mortal manifestations, but this should not be allowed to cloud the issue during the investigation of the phenomenon as such.

Ellis should also have been given to understand that it was his task to form his own opinion, and not to *adopt* different viewpoints at different times.

Mr. Cutten knew early in 1971 that Ellis was going to apply for an extension of his grant for another year as from September. In June Mr. Cutten published a highly critical review of Raudive's work. It was reasonable to assume that Ellis would find it very difficult to ignore the strong feelings of his Supervisor in regard to the Voice Phenomenon.

Mr. Cutten is as much entitled to his opinion as everybody else, but I doubt the wisdom of his agreeing to accept the position of Ellis' Supervisor. In the long run it does not matter much whether Ellis' final report decides one way or the other; those who have read his interim reports are already aware of his problems.

It was inevitable that David Ellis became aware of our dilemma. My main responsibility to the publishing house was to prevent any leaks to the newspapers at this stage of our investigations, however innocently dropped. I therefore suggested to David Ellis that he should sign an agreement with us under which we offered him the full text of the forthcoming book, including the reports by a number of experts, and any materials which might be relevant to his work. In return, Ellis undertook not to give any interviews to the press, radio or television before publication date of

Breakthrough without our agreement in advance. We also stipulated that his Report No. 3 which would contain a detailed analysis of Raudive's book was not to be published before publication of the book itself; however, we agreed to his discussing the book with his Supervisor.

Two more experiments followed on 4 February and 8 February. Neither yielded any remarkable results (with the exception of the latter when the Bang and Olufsen recorder went up in smoke).

It had become quite clear that we were not able to demonstrate the Voice Phenomenon publicly without asking Dr. Raudive to participate in an experiment. I was certainly not prepared to undertake such a task because I was technically not qualified to do so. I had to present *Breakthrough* to the general public; this in turn depended entirely on the validity of Raudive's claims, and our Chairman had by now made the position quite clear; I was to inform Dr. Raudive that we would probably drop *Breakthrough* unless he were prepared to come to England one week before publication and put himself at the disposal of the press and any experts who wished to examine his recording methods.

Dr. Raudive agreed without hesitation and he arrived on Monday, 22 March. I made the necessary preparations with representatives of the press for Monday, Tuesday and Thursday. On Friday, 26 March, Raudive would experiment with some physicists in a Faraday cage at Belling and Lee. No plans were made for Wednesday.

Two papers, *The Sunday Times* and *The Sunday Mirror*, showed great interest in the book. Unfortunately, we had to agree that *Breakthrough* did not lend itself to serialisation, but *The Sunday Mirror* offered to give major coverage to Raudive's work, subject to our agreeing to their conditions. First, they wanted an entire afternoon and evening for an exclusive experiment. *The Sunday Mirror* would appoint a senior journalist to cover the event, they would select their own engineers and recording experts, provide their own machinery and tapes and the experiment had to be carried out under the strict supervision of their engineers. Dr.

Raudive would not be allowed to handle any instruments and their reporter was to be completely in charge of the preceedings. We sent to the Features Editor, Mr. Cyril Kersh, a list of the guests we had invited to be present during the experiment on Tuesday. They included Sir Robert and Lady Mayer, Mr. Bearman, Joyce Morton, David Stanley, Malcolm Hughes, Mrs. Yanah Deavalow, and four members of our publishing house. We were not informed who the engineers would be, but Mr. Kersh told me that Ronald Maxwell would be in charge. Other arrangements included an evening (Monday) with a team from *Tomorrow's World* of the BBC and Mr. Graham Rose of *The Sunday Times*. For Thursday we had arranged an interview (not experiment) with *The News of the World*. A short interview with the religious correspondent of *The Sunday Telegraph* was fixed for Monday afternoon. It was through sheer lack of time and opportunity that we did not invite other newspapers; however, we prepared an extensive press release and informed them that Dr. Raudive was available to answer any questions on Wednesday and Friday evening. Although I shall be dealing with the press coverage later, it is interesting to note that I had sent an invitation to the Editor of *Psychic News* and offered both Mr. Barbanell or any representative of the paper the opportunity to come on all three days: Mr. Barbanell declined the offer. In retrospect, I see why; he wanted the experiments to be carried out strictly in accordance with our policy of not giving anybody the opportunity to level at us the criticism that Spiritualists had taken part, and thus allow reporters to describe an experiment as a seance. Mr. Barbanell and some members of his staff are well known for their psychic gifts, and he exercised a judgement on this occasion for which the publishers are grateful; it had not even occurred to us that the presence of a Spiritualist at our experiments might have given cause for the misrepresentation of facts. Personally, I regret that Mr. Barbanell did not meet Raudive or come to the controlled experiments. From what I have learned about him, he might have made a valuable contribution.

5

Publish and be Damned

A widely publicised launching of *Breakthrough* depended entirely on the outcome of the experiments carried out between 22 and 25 March '71. To put not too fine a point on this, the meeting at which Sir Robert Mayer would be present, was probably the most important, although he was prepared to accept any one of three successful experiments, as long as he could verify the findings with the independent press and scientific representatives. Sir Robert had informed me some weeks earlier that he would have to dissociate himself from the book if he was not satisfied with the Voice Phenomenon itself. This would, of course, have been the same as not publishing it. Although we had sent review copies to the press, I was at that time prepared to put publication of *Breakthrough* to the vote; I expected Colin Smythe to vote for publication, but I would have voted with Sir Robert Mayer, because his dissociation with a publishing venture by the firm of which he is Chairman, would have done far greater damage to us than dropping the publicity campaign. We could not have stopped reviews from appearing, but there would have been no radio and television interviews and our representatives would have been instructed not to carry the book any longer. In fairness to us, Sir Robert had also told me not to worry about any losses; he would take personal responsibility for them if things went wrong; eight thousand books had been printed; about one hundred review copies had gone out, and bookshops had already been sent their consignments. It is difficult to estimate the actual losses we would have incurred, but I was far more concerned about a possible disagreement, the first, among the board of our directors. Though I was very worried, I did not tell Colin Smythe of Sir Robert's strong feelings on the subject. His enthusiasm and positive planning of the various recording sessions have contributed much to their eventual outcome. Besides, if the experiments had turned out to be failures, there would have been time enough to explain the situation to him afterwards.

On Dr. Raudive's arrival I informed him of his time-table and told him that the proof of the pudding was in the eating. New experiments had to be carried out, and probably under conditions he might not appreciate or might positively dislike. He was in complete agreement and promised to do everything in his power to satisfy everybody. "However," he said, "I have prepared a press release which has to be translated into English." As Nadia Fowler was in Switzerland, I offered to translate his statement, I then discovered that it consisted of eight type-written pages; nevertheless I translated it, with Dr. Raudive discussing every single sentence with me. This took care of the first five hours of his stay. When I went up with him to his guestroom, we discovered to our horror that Rufus, my Great Dane, had found the open door and the bed too inviting to resist. He had settled on the bed, on top of Dr. Raudive's tape recorder; twelve stone is quite a weight and the machine was broken. I know it is silly, but this appeared to me a dreadful omen at the time. An emergency call to David Stanley brought him over, and he had the tape recorder repaired by Tuesday.

At six o'clock, the team from *Tomorrow's World* arrived, Mr. Andy Wiseman and Mr. Brian Johnson, both producers with considerable scientific background, and an assistant. We discussed the phenomenon at length; Mr. Wiseman, who is fluent in German and Russian, was able to do all the translating himself. On this occasion, I also played to Mr. Wiseman the tape of Monsignor O'Connor, and found Dr. Raudive's translation confirmed. At 8 o'clock we decided to start the experiment, although Graham Rose of *The Sunday Times* had not arrived. Half way through the recording Mr. Rose turned up, and the experiment was abandoned for the moment in order to explain some technical details to him. For the experiment, Dr. Raudive used my Ferguson tape recorder and a diode. The result was not bad; a number of voices had manifested themselves, some of them more clearly than others. There were the inevitable "Koste" and "Raudive" calls and the odd word here and there. Perhaps the most significant sentence (if two words justify the use of the word 'sentence'), was on the second recording. Throughout the playback of the first tape, both Graham Rose and Andy Wiseman showed their astonishment and called out "I buy this", whenever they heard one of the voices. If one of them heard "Koste" and the other agreed, he would say "I buy this". On the second tape we all could hear quite clearly the sentence "Buy Koste". To me this made sense, in so far as it appeared to be a direct response to a phrase which had been used frequently in reference to other voices. I was therefore disappointed when Graham Rose spelled it 'by Koste' in his article the following Sunday. Mr. Wiseman was quite impressed; he and Mr. Johnson explained that it was impossible to include a televised recording for Thursday night's programme, but showed serious interest in sending a team to Germany to make a documentary film at a later time. It had become obvious that controlled experiments involve a time-consuming period which does not make good television. Also, the problem of amplifying the voices in such a manner that the background noise was cut out completely, leaving the voices clear and audible to be picked up by a studio microphone for transmission, seemed impossible. However, both gentlemen assured me that they were absolutely satisfied about Dr. Raudive's sincerity and genuineness. Graham Rose arranged to telephone me during the week and clear up any queries he might have. This he did on Thursday morning. He read the article he had written and I was able to fill in dates and places. Thus I knew, or thought I knew, what would appear in *The Sunday Times;*

in order to give a correct account of my conversation with Graham to Dr. Raudive and Colin Smythe, I told him that I would tape the part when he read the article to me. On Sunday morning I hardly recognised the piece which appeared on the "Spectrum" page. Editors and sub-editors can, if they so wish, cut articles and reports even if they are by such seasoned journalists as Graham Rose, and I sometimes wonder why they bother to send an experienced man on a job when the end result looks as if it had been written by some junior reporter who, instead of going to be present at an experiment, has gone to watch a football match instead. What I saw printed in *The Sunday Times*, bore little relation to the original article. I am sorry about this because Graham Rose certainly seemed to have grasped a number of points which had escaped many other observers. In the course of the evening Mr. Rose had asked about experiments in a Faraday cage and I told him that such an experiment was planned for the following Friday. I offered to let him have the result on Friday night.

In his last paragraph Graham Rose points out that an experiment in a Faraday cage was an absolute necessity and that these voices could perhaps be explained as pick-ups from low frequency transmitters operated by the C.I.A., an equally startling theory. On Friday evening I had been able to assure *The Sunday Times* that the C.I.A. could not be blamed for the Voice Phenomena as the experiment in a screened laboratory had been successful; alas, the article had already been set up.

On Tuesday morning I received a telephone call from *The Sunday Mirror*, informing me that they had booked two recording experts from Pye Records Ltd., the chief engineer in charge of recordings and the chief engineer for recording equipment, and that I should have a room ready so that they could set up their machines and other instruments in time to check it before the actual experiment would start.

At 4 p.m. Ronald Maxwell arrived; shortly afterwards the photographer; Mr. Ray Prickett of Pye arrived at 4.30 p.m.

and Mr. Kenneth Attwood about 10 minutes later. Mr. Maxwell had not met either of them previously.

At 5.30 the invited guests and the *Mirror* investigators assembled for a general discussion. Only then did I introduce Dr. Raudive to them. The next hour was taken up with an animated discussion during which Ronald Maxwell and the two engineers cleared a number of points for the experiment which would follow shortly. Messrs. Attwood and Prickett had brought with them a considerable amount of equipment which they installed in the dining room; of particular interest was a diode, specially built for this experiment, which would show even the smallest electro-magnetic input on a very sensitive scale. A recording machine with oscillator and additional controls as well as protected tapes and a multitude of electronic gadgets soon turned our dining room into a laboratory. Most of the instruments were set up on the dining room table which I had covered with green baize. The seating was arranged by Mr. Maxwell; Mr. Ray Prickett was in charge of the actual recording procedure and monitored the oscillator throughout the evening. Mr. Attwood took charge of the other instruments, including the diode with a built-in frequency changer. Dr. Raudive was seated between Ronald Maxwell on his right and myself acting as interpreter on his left, with Ken Attwood on my left and Ray Prickett with his recording machines at one end of the table. Sir Robert Mayer sat on the left of Mr. Prickett. At the other end of the table were Mr. Bearman, who had set up his own tape recorder with microphone, on his left was David Stanley and on his right Lady Mayer. Four more guests were seated in between the two groups. We had decided that only twelve persons at any given time should be in the room, but that the two electronics engineers, Dr. Raudive, myself and Sir Robert Mayer should remain in their places throughout the evening. During the actual recording Ray Prickett wore earphones, and four more sets were available for Ken Attwood, Dr. Raudive, Ronald Maxwell and myself. Before the recording session started, Ken Attwood explained the function of some of the electronic gadgets; he assured us that every precaution had been taken to prevent freak pick-ups of any kind and that the possibility of picking up random high and low frequency transmissions had also been excluded. In other words, these controls would make it completely impossible to pick up anything—unless, of course, Raudive's theory was right. Ken Attwood also made it quite clear that he did not expect any voices to manifest themselves, and he was vigorously endorsed by Ray Prickett. As a diode recording cannot be interfered with by voices in the room, ordinary conversation could continue. However, a microphone recording of this particular conversation which went on during the next ten minutes was also made. Therefore it has been possible to co-ordinate what was said at any given time with the recordings which appeared on the controlled tape with a diode input.

According to his method, Raudive invited all of us to state our name and, if we wanted to, ask any of our departed friends to communicate. This caused embarrassment on the part of some guests. Sir Robert Mayer took this opportunity of challenging the many "Koste", "Raudive" and other personal messages, which seemed to dominate most of Raudive's recordings. "I am 92 years old," he said, "and most of my contemporaries are dead. Would it not be reasonable to assume that I, or my wife for that matter, should be getting far more messages tonight than anybody here? One of our dearest friends, the late Artur Schnabel, would never miss such an opportunity of getting in touch with us."

Sir Robert spoke with some emotion, and it was clear to me that he was prepared to have the entire question of the genuineness of the voices cleared up here and now. He was not willing to accept a communication that was limited to Dr. Raudive, and he also made it clear that Artur Schnabel would certainly not talk to him or his wife in Latvian. Ken Attwood intervened and pointed out to Sir Robert that it was rather immaterial to him in what language communications would take place; as far as he was concerned, no single sound wave could possibly penetrate their control devices. Although I have reconstructed here a coherent conversation between Sir Robert and Ken Attwood, there was another interruption as soon as Sir Robert started to speak. This took place when the counter recorded 90 revolutions. The control device on the diode suddenly began to register electro-magnetic impulses. I saw it quite clearly and tried to draw Attwood's attention to it, but when he looked the indicator was steady again. However, he did not move his eyes from the control for the rest of the experiment. Mr. Prickett, who monitored the oscillator, had not noticed anything. At revolution 250, the control device suddenly registered a strong series of signals. Ken Attwood was very excited, assuring us that this just could not happen. Prickett, on the other hand, still checking the oscillator, called out that not a single signal was being registered at his end. Ronald Maxwell, I myself and one or two others, among them David Stanley, now watched the control device attached to the diode. There was no doubt that at regular intervals signals were recorded. Attwood changed the frequency, but the signals were still recorded. Of course, the observations by the two engineers in charge of the controls contradict each other. How was it possible that one device registered signals and the other did not? Both devices were synchronised and in perfect harmony. However, whether or not any voices had been recorded, remained to be seen. The recording lasted 18 minutes and not ten, as we had planned. With all the excitement going on, we completely forget to watch the time. The playback was organised by Ronald Maxwell. A second tape recorder was brought in and the earphones connected. Ray Prickett transferred the tape with the diode recording and Ronald Maxwell got his pad ready to write down whatever might appear on the tape. Attwood, Raudive, Prickett, Maxwell and myself used the earphones, whilst Sir Robert and three other members of the party sat opposite and watched the proceedings. A spare set of earphones was used by them whenever something interesting had occurred.

We had agreed to prepare an over-all record of the 18 minute tape first, Maxwell indicating the revolution number and place where a voice appeared. However, no time was wasted on long interpretations at this time. After a first examination which lasted about two hours, we had identified over two hundred places where voices were discernible. Twenty-seven voices were so clear that Ken Attwood suggested a powerful loudspeaker might be connected to the tape recorder instead of the earphones, so that everybody could listen.

As the entire procedure lasted until the early hours of the morning, it is impossible to recall everything that happened; besides I doubt if I could really describe the excitement and the feelings of all those present. Sir Robert and Lady Mayer seemed to be favoured with personal messages, and, perhaps not surprisingly, by Artur Schnabel. He spoke in German, the language in which he had always spoken to both of them. On revolution 86 a man's voice called out "Artur" at 251 the words "nanti(?) wir danken" which means "nanti(?) we thank you"; on 333 up to 347 "Artur—wir sind hier", meaning "Artur—we are here"; on 480 starts a long sentence of which unfortunately, only two words were clearly understandable, the first one "Artur" and the last one "Barbirolli". (Sir John Barbirolli who had just died, was a close friend of Sir Robert and Lady Mayer.)

During the recording at revolution 226, Mr. Victor Bearman spoke; on playback of the tape, at revolution 232 a man's voice calls out "Kurla"; this is Latvian for "you are deaf". I really cannot vouch for the translation, as I don't speak Latvian myself; however, I am prepared to accept Raudive's translation. One thing is certain, everybody except Mr. Bearman understood quite clearly "Kurla". Mr. Bearman wears a hearing aid and suffers from deafness. On revolution 520 the name "Malcolm" was called out. On revolution 542 a voice called "Mother". Among the other voices which could be heard quite clearly were: "Raudive" three times, "Kosti" or "Koste", Raudive's nickname for Konstantin, twice, and "Tekle" the name of Raudive's

61

sister, appeared three times.

After the initial excitement, it was the turn of the two innocent engineers, Ray Prickett and Ken Attwood, to explain their failure to prevent voices from manifesting themselves. Prickett was obviously troubled by the events. He could not explain the voices and began theorising with David Stanley on very complicated technical points. Ken Attwood, on the other hand, suggested that it was useless to hold an inquest into why the voices had got through, and that it was far more important to break the mystery one way or the other or to see whether the quality of the voices could be improved.

Sir Robert's reaction was brief and to the point. "Peter", he said to me, "we publish! If the chief engineers of Pye are baffled, I don't see any reason why we should not present this remarkable discovery to the general public." Ronald Maxwell immediately interviewed Sir Robert and asked for his reaction. I managed to listen in to most of the conversations; Sir Robert's first reaction had been one of shock: "After 92 years it looks as if I have to adjust myself to some form of activity after I have left this earth. Perhaps I even get the chance of organising some celestial children's concerts," he said jokingly, "but I am relieved at the thought that eternity does not mean being condemned to eternal inactivity. At least this was the first thought which came into my mind. I need some more time to adjust my thoughts to what I have witnessed here tonight." To Lady Mayer the demonstration was "only confirmation of what I have believed and known for a long time. However, this material proof is exciting and challenging and the Churches should take up the challenge science provides them with."

Ken Attwood and Ray Prickett promised to send their report to Ronald Maxwell within 48 hours.

There was no doubt in anybody's mind that the evening had been a great success.

This only left Thursday for the interview with Alan Whittaker of *The News of the World*. No doubt, Dr. Raudive was tired and exhausted from Tuesday's experiment; Alan Whittaker, like Ronald Maxwell, writes for a large readership to whom philosophical and theological implications are meaningless; they want to know whether it will be possible in the near future to "dial M for Mother", or if anybody could get in touch with Aunt Flo. Dr. Raudive began by explaining how bored he was with popular newspapers and how he much preferred to discuss the philosophy of post-mortal existence. I felt I had to tone down much of what he said because Alan Whittaker might have taken offence. I was greatly relieved when after four hours Alan Whittaker seemed to have enough information to get on with. Something different had caught the imagination of Brian Thomas, *The News of the World* photographer, at whose insistence I had allowed Rufus to remain in the room. Perhaps I had never given much thought to Rufus' strange behaviour before, but whenever he had been in the room during the playback of voices, he appeared particularly restless. He would suddenly bark at some 'intruder', his bristles would stand up and he would make the same noises I would normally associate with a stranger approaching the house. I had already noticed that these barks always coincided with voices on a tape—hardly audible to me, and I had almost come to associate Rufus' barks with a voice on the tape; yet I don't think I had ever consciously linked the two factors. It was Brian Thomas who drew my attention to it during one of the Raudive playbacks. He took a photograph of Rufus listening to the tape. From then on I have watched him; but, as always in such cases, Rufus seemed to lose interest as soon as he was aware of being watched. Jennifer Cross later wrote a long feature article in *The Bucks Free Press* under the heading *"DOES RUFUS HOLD THE SECRET OF THE VOICES FROM THE DEAD?"* The idea seems preposterous, but is it really so far fetched? Is it not possible that the voices are more audible to him than to us? I have never tested this theory under controlled conditions as I doubt very much whether Rufus, who has a will of his own, would even condescend to collaborate! However, I have watched him unobtrusively many times, and so have others. My psychological studies have always been concerned with human beings; I know therefore very little about animal psychology, other than what any dog owner learns from his pet, but certain aspects of his behaviour are remarkable. He does not show any sign of interest in the radio or gramophone. He certainly likes watching television sometimes, but he does not react or bark. Yet with a tape recorder in the room and probably bored with the little attention he gets, he seems to respond to noises which we find difficult to locate. Be this as it may, some weeks later Professor Bender's report arrived and it is worthwhile mentioning here that the tests with the voice printer have clearly indicated that these voices appear to manifest themselves on the fringe of our own frequency range of hearing. But more of that later. It is therefore reasonable to assume that Rufus hears these voices before and better than we do. In contrast to the Great Dane, Colin Smythe's black Labrador, a most efficient and reliable guard dog, shows no interest in the voice recordings whatever. She neither barks nor moves her head. For all I know, she does not hear any voices. Somehow, Rufus seems to have captured the imagination of many reporters and photographers, but is it not possible that he holds at least part of the secret of the voices? Is it not possible that his astute hearing and recognition of some familiar sound caused him to react as he would do with human strangers? I have spoken to many friends who own dogs; they all can relate a story about their pets showing signs of fear,timidity or aggression for no apparent reason. Still, I don't think it would help the research into the Voice Phenomena much if we were side-tracked at this moment by expecting the answers to be given by the animal world.

On 27 March, Dr. Raudive was taken by David Ellis to Enfield, for an experiment in the Radio-Frequency-Screened Laboratory of Belling and Lee Ltd. Mr. Ralph Lovelock, the electronics engineer and physicist, was there and Raudive met Mr. Peter Hale, who is one of the five leading experts in electronic screen suppression in the West; he is certainly

Britain's foremost expert.

On their return I spoke to Raudive and Ellis about the experiment. Raudive was quite happy and even excited about the results, saying that at least 20 voices had been recorded and analysed afterwards. Mr. Ellis told me that there were 'a lot of questions unanswered', and that Peter Hale had said (before the experiment started, in fact two days' before the meeting on 27 March) that in his (Hale's) opinion, Dr. Raudive's voices originated from normal radio signals, i.e. the 'Luxembourg Effect'; the modulation of carrier waves by uneven reflections in the ionosphere.

Naturally, I was anxious to hear what Mr. Hale had to say after the experiment in a laboratory which was specifically designed to screen out such radio signals. Although far fewer voices were recorded on this occasion than, for example, on Tuesday evening, the experiment has been significant to the experts. Bearing in mind what Mr. Hale is purported to have said to Mr. Ellis on 24 March, no voices should have been recorded at all, but they were recorded and under strictly controlled conditions. We should remember that the firm of Belling and Lee, and especially Mr. Hale, are concerned with the testing of the most sophisticated electronic equipment. His opinion and judgement are sought by those responsible for the defence of this country and by the leading researchers in the world. Any experiment in which Mr. Hale takes part, and upon which he comments must therefore be conducted under conditions which do not allow possible charges of negligence or carelessness.

I have so far avoided giving any technical explanations which require special knowledge but I consider it important to quote a few lines from Mr. Ellis' report. This passage may help those with some understanding of electronics to appreciate the experiment better; as for those who, like myself, look upon any electronic gadget as some kind of 20th century witchcraft, it is confirmation that experts have been baffled once again.

"Mr Hale had set up a signal generator plus aerial and a sensitive radio receiver, which could feed a signal to

a tape recorder. Mr. Lovelock adjusted the radio apparatus: the signal transmitted and received was an unmodulated (approx.) 1.4 MHz and the signal fed to the tape recorder was therefore made up of noises from the signal generator and from the radio amplifier. The microphone was used for giving introductory details and announcements, and for asking the Spirits how they were getting on . . . .
I supplied a brand new BASF 3" LP tape for the experiment, and recordings were made on the whole of tracks 1 and 4 at 3 3/4 i.p.s. When the tapes were played back, Dr. Raudive detected several voices in the microphone sections, one of which was quite clear. It seemed to say "KUR RAUDI" (Latvian: 'Where is Raudi?') It is also possible that there are some more faint voices in the radio section, but the tape has not yet been properly analysed . . . ."

So much for Ellis' report on the procedure. In the light of these results, Mr. Hale wrote us a letter from which he allowed us to quote to the press.

"From the results we obtained last Friday, something is happening which I cannot explain in normal physical terms."

I did not accompany Raudive to Enfield that day because I had much work to do for the forthcoming publication of *Breakthrough*. At lunchtime I had a meeting with Ronald Maxwell and later with the Features Editor of *The Sunday Mirror*. The Picture Editor had sent a series of photographs to the Editorial Department, and Ronald and I looked through them and we discussed which might be suitable for Sunday's article. He told me that a three-page feature was envisaged. When Mr. Kersh, the Features Editor joined us he jokingly asked whether the two engineers of Pye were on our payroll. Continuing in this lighthearted vein, he suggested that everybody on Tuesday night must have been completely drunk to accept that the dead were talking on tape recorders. He then got down to business, and we continued discussing the story and the likely impact it was going to make on their readers. The report from Pye had been received and Maxwell told me that they could offer no explanation whatever for the Voice Phenomenon. Of course that was what *The Sunday Mirror* had wanted, a definite statement from electronics experts of their choice testifying that no trickery had been employed. Maxwell then said that he would be in his office on Saturday morning, and if any more questions should arise, he would telephone me at my home.

From the *Mirror* building I drove straight to the B.B.C. studio and recorded two interviews, one to be broadcast at 8 a.m. on Sunday morning in a religious programme and another one for Mr. Jack de Manio's *Today* programme on Monday morning.

On Saturday morning Ronald Maxwell telephoned and asked me for details about one or two guests who were in the photographs. When I enquired how he was getting on, he told me that the article was already being set. Dr. Raudive left London at noon for Switzerland.

In view of the expected press coverage of *Breakthrough,* Colin Smythe and I decided to go to the BEA air terminal late on Saturday night and buy a copy of all the Sunday papers. Most papers carried something about the Voice Phenomenon with the exception of *The Sunday Mirror*: I was certain I had picked up some freak copy with the centre pages missing. When I realised that this was not so, I wondered whether this early edition might have left the printers before the article had been completed. The copy we obtained from our local newsagent on Sunday morning made no reference to Tuesday's experiment either. I telephoned Ronald Maxwell at his home and got him out of bed. "You must be joking" he said, "I left the office in the afternoon and I personally saw the pages in proof." He looked at his own copy, and there was a long silence at his end. "I just don't know what could have happened, but I will find out and ring you back," were his last words and he hung up. I have never found out the exact details of what happened, but Ronald Maxwell told me that after he had left, the Editor-in-Chief refused to have the story in the paper. As he has absolute power in what goes in and what does not, there was nothing anybody could do, least of all, Kersh or Maxwell. The experiment which had been arranged and paid for by *The Sunday Mirror* had yielded results which did not please the man at the top. I know that they both tried once again, to produce another story on the subject a week later; this time Maxwell had collected information and statements from leading scientists, among them Mr. Peter Hale. Again, the Editor-in-Chief refused to publish the article. Naturally I was disappointed, but looking back at it, I am very grateful to the staff of *The Sunday Mirror*: for it was at their insistence that an experiment had been arranged in the first place, and objective and independent experts had carried out an investigation at its expense. But it was *The Sunday Mirror's* loss not to print this exclusive story. After the wide national coverage of the Voice Phenomenon, during the week after publication, I received a complaint from George Topley of *The Bucks Free Press,* asking me why local papers had not been invited to any of the experiments. I explained that this had been simply a case of 'no room at the inn'; however, to make amends, I handed him a complete transcript of the events which took place on Tuesday, 23 March, and he wrote a most fascinating article under the heading *VOICES FROM THE DEAD AT GERRARDS CROSS.* The result was a tremendous response from *Free Press* readers; and I was confirmed in my opinion that *The Sunday Mirror* had missed out on a coup.

On Monday, 29 March, *Breakthrough* was launched, and with it one of the greatest controversies in the field of parapsychology and electronics.

6

The First Confrontation

Shortly after the publication of *Breakthrough, The Daily Telegraph* featured an article under the headline: ALMOST EVERY TECHNOLOGICAL ADVANCE HITHERTO MADE BY CIVIL- ISATION HAS BEEN DISCARDED BEFOREHAND AS A PRACTICAL IMPOSSIBILITY. The British science philosopher Arthur C. Clarke explained that such foolish judgements had invar- iably been advanced by persons claiming expert knowledge. Clarke continues: "When an elderly and distinguished scientist tells you that something is impossible, he is almost certainly wrong. The experts can spot all the difficulties, but lack the imagination and vision to see how they can be overcome. The layman's ignorant optimism turns out, in the long run—and often in the short run—to be nearer the truth." Among the many examples Clarke recalls that British enthusiasts in the 1930s did much of the theoretical groundwork necessary for a moon shot, but serious scientists dismissed them as cranks; after their first successful attempt with their flying machine, the Wright Brothers at once contacted the newspapers, but editors refused to print this "ridiculous story"; in 1920 *The New York Times* attacked Robert Goddard for putting forward the idea that rockets would work in the vacuum of space; "he seems to lack the knowledge about gravity ladled out daily in our high schools" they wrote. This fascinating and well written article highlighted precisely the kind of reaction I found among some people who claimed to have expert knowledge in the field of electronics. The real experts, however, (although some of them are elderly and distinguished) showed a remarkable sense of reality and optimism. Professor Hans Bender, Director of the Institute of Psychology, University of Freiburg, stated as far back as 1968 that the discovery of the Voice Phenomenon was probably as important, if not more so, than the discovery of nuclear physics. Peter Hale, in his statement showed true honesty when he said that he could not explain the Phenomenon in normal physical terms. Unfortunately, honesty usually makes bad television and dull copy for a newspaper. In science, especially physics, nothing is ever absolutely certain. No scientist worth his salt will use the word 'absolute'; unfortunately, interviewers and reporters are not satisfied with phrases like 'highly probable' or 'it looks as if . . . .'. It is not so much a question of not telling the whole truth as of allowing factual statements to be made which are scientifically untenable.

On 30 April, I received Professor Bender's report which was published by his Institute: another report by Dipl.Ing. Jochem Sotscheck of the Central Office for Telegraphic Technology, Berlin and Director of the Research Group for Acoustics, made up the second part of the report on the 'voices'. We had long known that this report was in preparation, and Dr. Raudive had promised to deliver Professor Bender's contribution some nine months earlier for inclusion in the book. Ironically, it arrived on publication day. (The reasons for the delay will become clearer in a later chapter when I deal with Friedrich Jürgenson, the discoverer of the Voice Phenomenon.) Both reports were in German and of a highly technical nature. Professor Bender's long and detailed report ends with a brief analysis in English:

"As an initial approach the Freiburg Institute in 1964 made an exploratory experiment to determine whether the voice phenomena were normally explainable or evidence of paranormal effects. A second examination with better technical equipment in May 1970 made the *paranormal hypothesis of the origin of the voice phenomena highly probable.* The analysis of the sounds with visible-speech-diagrams (a voice printer:) proved to be very helpful for the objective documentation of the supposed meaning."

This is as exciting and positive a report as one could possibly get. Professor Bender was satisfied that it was highly probable these voices on tape have a paranormal origin. Of course, he was not alone in his findings: among the researchers were the physicist Dr. F. Karger of the Max Planck Institute, Munich, the Director of the German Institute for Field-Physics, Dipl.Phys.B.Heim and his sound engineer W. Schott, Dr. J. Keil of the Institute of Psychology, University of Tasmania and a number of technical and scientific assistants.

Mr. Sotscheck's report on the tests with a voice printer testifies to "most encouraging results" and he makes a number of technical suggestions for further tests, for example, that recordings should be made which would exclude 'echo' effects because of difficulties arising from 'disturbing' signals which interfere with the 'useful' signals.

There is, however, an interesting sentence in the conclusion of Bender's report which also applies to Sotscheck's: "The hypothesis that the voice phenomena originate from sources indicating the existence of life after death is a *'Cura Posterior'*. The most pressing task of parapsychological research is to clear the possibility of a psychokinetic origin".

This simply means that Professor Bender wants first to explore the possibility of the human mind (i.e. that of the experimenter) being responsible for the voices, and he looks on Jürgenson's and Raudive's claim that these are the voices of people who have left this earth as a solution which should come later and after his theory has been found impossible. Jürgenson and Raudive, both highly qualified men in the academic sense, are really 'laymen' in the opinion of many of the professors and experts who have taken up the study of the voices. Arthur C. Clarke's statement that "the layman's optimism turns out to be nearer the truth", may well apply here, and Professor Bender is the first person to acknowledge that possibility; all the same, as far as actual proof is concerned, no scientist will ever stick his neck out and say: "this is absolutely so!"

I was highly delighted to have Bender's report to quote from during a series of interviews with radio and television. However, I soon realised that the fact of the report not being actually part of the book was held against me; critics suggested I was cheating, introducing supplementary evidence—which I thought was rather a strange attitude.

My first encounter with 'hostile' critics took place on BBC 2 *Late Night Line-Up* on 26 April 1971. When I arrived at the studio, Sheridan Morley introduced me to my 'opponents', as he put it. They were Rosalind Heywood, a Vice-President of the S.P.R. and Gordon Turner, a well-known healer and medium. Much has been said about biased interviews and slanted reporting by the Corporation. Although I have participated in about 20 programmes on the Voice Phenomenon transmitted by BBC Radio and BBC Television, I can say that not one single interviewer tried to trick me or was biased. One or two may have said to me before the programme: "Are you sure this is one the level?" or "Mind you, I just cannot believe this myself", but during the interviews or debates they were completely unbiased and fair. Sheridan Morley, for example, when mentioning to me that he gathered both Mrs. Heywood and Mr. Turner were going to give me a rough time, offered to take my side. I asked him not to do so, and Mr .Morley assured me that he would certainly watch that I would get my fair share of the debate. It is not Mr. Morley's fault that this turned out to be impossible. Mrs .Heywood was determined to have her say and knew that no gentleman would dare stop her. Morley, Turner and myself were plainly out-talked. Mrs. Heywood is a most charming lady; after the programme she apologised to me for having taken up so much time, and I gladly accept her apology because apart from her charm, Mrs. Heywood possesses a delightful sense of humour. Unfortunately, her arguments during the programme were more dialectic and rhetorical than sound.

For a start, she considered it highly unfair that I should use Professor Bender's report as evidence, because it was not in the book. Secondly, when I pointed out that the leading physicists and electronics engineers had carried out many experiments just to eliminate one recording method in preference to another, she retorted: "Over the weekend I rang up three electronic experts, they all said that they could think of 12 different ways in which these voices could have occured." When I referred to the Perrott-Warrick Studentship of Mr. David Ellis, she told me that I could not mention this here because she knew all about that; besides, she was associated with the awarding council, "this studentship has been going for years, it's nothing new." Mrs. Heywood also told me that she had read only parts of the book because she had only been told over the weekend that she was to appear on Monday night's programme.

Gordon Turner's argument seemed to have upset many viewers. For the first time, the question of danger was raised, and problems arising from some of the speech contents. However, it is important to remember that Turner started the discussion in an aggressive mood, not so much because of the Voice Phenomenon but because he had been asked to comment first on a programme that had preceded *Late Night Line-Up*. The "Play For Today" was about a phoney medium who with an associate extorted money from recently bereaved persons. In the introduction to our programme, Gordon was referred to as "A spiritual healer and practising medium", and Tony Bilbow went on to introduce the Voice Phenomenon as the latest method of communicating with the dead. There followed a recorded voice, which purported to come from Winston Churchill, and Mr. Bilbow continued: "Anyhow, if it works, the benefits to mankind could be enormous, from Plato advising Mr. Heath to Shakespeare dictating a 'Play For Today'."

The Churchill voice, and especially its interpretations, have caused more controversy than any other recording among the 72,000 collected by Raudive. In my Preface to *Breakthrough* I deal at some length with the author's linguistic talents; may it suffice to say that Dr. Raudive is not multi-lingual in the sense I understand it. Circumstances beyond his control have forced this learned man to change his country of residence several times. His vocabulary is vast and drawn from many languages. His native language is Latvian with Russian as a second mother tongue; followed by Swedish ,German, Spanish. He also knows some French, English and Italian. It would be unfair to expect him to understand the more subtle points of the English language and its pronunciation. When he sent us the 'Churchill' recording, it was classified as in English, Latvian and Swedish: *"Te Mac-Cloo, mej dream, my dear, yes"*. At the time it was so insignificant that we never bothered to listen to it carefully. After constant pressure by Dr. Raudive, we agreed in January '71 to have a record cut of suitable voice samples. It was then that we listened to the recording of Churchill's voice and made it out to say: "Hear, Mark you, make believe, my dear, yes". I remember Nadia Fowler, the translator, suggesting that anything would sound better than the pidgin English on the original transcript. Michael Smythe of Vista Records undertook to cut three thousand discs and, because of the shortage of time, he and Nadia Fowler prepared an English commentary on the lines of Raudive's German record. This particular voice, with commentary by Nadia Fowler, was also played on Jack De Manio's programme earlier in the month. Three days later I received a letter from Mr. J. C. Burley, an Engineering Consultant, who told me that he had listened carefully to that voice and that our interpretation was incorrect. What the man's voice (purporting to be Winston Churchill) said was: "Mark you, make thee mightier yet"—a quotation from "Land of Hope and Glory".

Immediately after the recording had been played, and before Sheridan Morley could mention the alternative interpretation, Gordon Turner made the wittiest remark I have heard on any programme concerning the Voice Phenomenon: "This is obviously one of Churchill's less important speeches which he saved to broadcast from the other side".

The question how meaningful and relevant the taped messages are is very important, and I shall some back to it in a later chapter. Gordon Turner's main criticism was directed against the banality of the Voice Phenomenon as a whole. "Let me tell you the level of this: it is the level of people playing about at a party with a ouija board where you push it around and get messages."

I pointed out to him that he could not dismiss the work of so many scientists and the research results by just comparing it with a ouija board, and Gordon gave me the reason for his opinion: "I am convinced that there has been and is communication with a spiritual world. Now, if *Breakthrough* is true, then all the messages that we have received, all that information that has been gathered in over a hundred years, becomes utter nonsense."

Whether Gordon Turner intended to do so or not, at this moment he had forced an issue, which in the words of Professor Bender is a 'cura posterior'; something that cannot possibly be explained in the near future and certainly not on a twenty minute programme. In other words, he challenged that either the work of the scientists was false and deceitful or Spiritualism, as we know it, was nonsense.

It appears that *Late Night Line-Up* is watched by most interviewers and producers of other programmes, because during subsequent television and radio discussions, almost the first question I was asked concerned the hostility of the Spiritualists. Of course, it had never occured to me that the Spiritualists were particularly hostile, nor did I see any reason for hostility .I had always maintained that the Voice Phenomenon was a problem primarily for the scientists, secondly for the psychologists, thirdly for the theologians and finally for our own common sense which would have to decide which arguments put forward by the 'experts' carried sufficient weight to convince. I have never looked upon the 'voices' as rivals of mediums nor as a threat to Spiritualism.

7

The Spiritualists and the Voices

It is mostly due to Britain's largest newspaper for Spiritualists, *Psychic News*, that the Voice Phenomenon was presented to the Spiritualists in this country in an objective manner. I regret that this paper is not more widely read, especially by people who are genuinely concerned with the question of life after death, although they might not adhere to the teachings of Spiritualism as such. I am neither a Spiritualist nor a member of any organisation or society concerning itself with psychic research. My beliefs are neither orthodox nor radical. On most questions I consult my conscience in preference to following a dogma. For the last two years I have taken to reading *Psychic News* regularly. I find it interesting and informative, no more and no less. Had it not been for the completely unbiased attitude taken by this paper and its Editor, Maurice Barbanell, the controversy over the Voice Phenomenon might have become a bitter and unpleasant episode. For something like ten weeks, a substantial part of the paper was given over to the supporters and opponents of *Breakthrough*. On 3 April, the entire front page was given to comments from the national press; the following number carried on the right hand side of the front page Gordon Turner's review of the book: "I am not convinced voices come from discarnate entities"—on the other half, the editor had extracted parts of my Preface to *Breakthrough* and headed the article (as prominently as the review) ' "I

heard 'dead' mother speak on tape"—says former sceptic.'
And in the next eight editions everybody had his say,
scientists, engineers, Spiritualists and those who just wanted
to get their opinion on record. *Psychic News* also covered
the problem of 'banality' in great detail, and many suggestions and opinions published in the paper have been of
great help to the scientists who are still concerned with
progress in this project. My only 'live' encounter with a
Spiritualist audience took place on 1 August at the Head-
quarters of the Spiritualist Association of Great Britain. In
April I had agreed to their request to give a lecture, but
my commitments made it impossible to do so earlier. I am
flattered that so many people came to listen to me and I
am sorry that a great number could not be admitted because
the hall was packed above capacity. The lecture lasted for
about ninety minutes; although I am quite accustomed to
speaking to large audiences, on that particular evening I
was made very nervous. The chairman of the meeting
appeared to have been briefed rather badly about the
speaker. As I walked into the lecture hall, an organ was
playing 'Ave Maria' by Gounod; the chairman led me to
the platform and assured me that the lights would be
dimmed in a moment. Then he proceeded to pull the
heavy velvet crtains, much to the dismay of the audience.
"Do you want a spot light on you?" he asked me, and when
I told him that I wanted neither a spotlight, nor the
curtains drawn nor the lights dimmed, he got very upset.
"But will they come through, my friend?", he asked. I was
somewhat at a loss. Of course, when the gentleman introduced me, I realised that he was expecting a demonstration.
He asked the audience to be specially quiet so as not to
disturb the unseen friends who would now speak to me
through this marvellous invention, the tape recorder. I am
sorry if I appeared a little puzzled, cutting the chairman
of the meeting short and putting the record straight. The
lecture was followed by a discussion, a somewhat disappointing experience, which prompted the editor of *Spiritualist
News* to write in his column:

F

"I was appalled to hear so called Spiritualists ask questions which displayed abysmal ignorance about our subject. When we are privileged to listen to lectures given by intellectuals let us endeavour to consider that everyone is entitled to their own opinions. Particularly when these opinions have been reached after intensive analysis. One chap stood up and accused the speaker of 'ignorance'. He added 'You have a long way to go before you can fully understand about such matters . . . . we Spiritualists already understand all about voices on tape.'

Listening to his comments, I wanted to hide my face! In any case questions were invited. Not biased opinion and an exposure of obvious lack of knowledge. Everyone keeps telling me that we have intelligent folk who can 'deal' with the scientists. I was disappointed to find that not one of them was in the audience."

I think Alex Owler was a little harsh with the audience. On the other hand, the fact that Spiritualists have newspapers like *Psychic News* and *Spiritualist News* and editors like Maurice Barbanell and Alex Owler, is, to me as an outsider, a sign of a healthy state of affairs! In this connection I must mention the quarterly magazine *Light,* published by the College of Psychic Studies and edited by Julian Duguid. The College of Psychic Studies, as does the S.P.R., claims an open minded attitude to any paranormal or psychic phenomenon. It is, however, fair to say that the C.P.S. adopts a positive approach and allows the views of its experts to be represented proportionally to the consensus of opinion. Hence, the Summer 1971 edition of *Light* carried four contributions of which Mr. Bearman's and Dr. Crookall's came out strongly in favour of the Phenomenon being para-normal; Mr. P. Beard was cautious and demanded more concerted research efforts before being prepared to commit himself, and Mr. N. Gaythorpe felt that there was no place in serious psychical research for irresponsible conclusions of the sort reached in the book. Robert Crookall, B.Sc.(Psychology), Ph.D., D.Sc., probably the most highly qualified scientist working in the field of psychical research, concluded the debate: "It will be evident that I regard Dr. Raudive's book as correctly titled."

Since then, subsequent editions of *Light* carried more contributions from Physicists, Psychologists and other qualified scientists, all taking issue with Norman Gaythorpe. The commendable attitude taken by the College can be summed up in the words of the magazine editor, Julian Duguid:

"There is no doubt whatever that these voices do appear on tape recorders. Believer and sceptic are agreed upon that. The question is how? Are they primitive astral jokers, as Paul Beard suggests? Or something else? Is the whole thing electronic nonsense, as Norman Gaythorpe says quite roundly? It is not the business of a completely non-electronic editor to take sides. It is his job to let everyone have their say. But I would suggest that there is room for a fruitful discussion between these four reviewers and any readers who may have strong views on this very important matter. After all, this is not a simple request for belief in spirits. It is a statement that messages come in a certain way . . . . and a scientific way at that. It is unreasonable to expect a scientist to accept such a revolutionary view until he has checked it from all angles.

Such a dialogue could begin by the believers asking the sceptics to devise experiments which would cut out the grounds of their scepticism. An electronics friend of mine said he would like to see experiments carried out at the bottom of a coal-mine or else in the middle of the Pacific Ocean.

Light has now performed its most pleasant duty in throwing the matter wide open. Let the dialogue begin."

The initial controversy started with Gordon Turner's remark that Voice Phenomena and Spiritualism were incompatible. I must therefore deal with the reasons he gives, 'danger' and 'abuse'. This, as Gordon has accepted, is not restricted to the Voice Phenomenon but applies to the entire field of psychic research. Of course, such voices could be abused; in that lies the danger. There is not a single invention which man has not learned to abuse: the telephone, television, the printed word and purely technological inventions such as the aeroplane and the motor car. The tape recorder is quite harmless and so are the electronic voices, unless deliberate or careless misinterpretation of sentences or words shows them to be otherwise. I do not deny that inexperience in dealing with electronic voices can also cause distress and therefore constitute a danger. So far only one case has become known to me: a young man wrote to me and I was able to discuss with him the points in question. At my request he furnished us with the tape which, in his opinion contained a threatening message. I have listened to it carefully, and so have some friends, all experienced in the playback method. The voice was there all right; independently four listeners established beyond a shadow of doubt what the voice said: "If you want to talk to him you have to talk to him now" and not, as the young man believed "If you want to talk to your Gran, we will torture her now". The case history is simple: the young man's grandmother had recently died and he tried to communicate with her, asking for her by name. As he was using the microphone method, I was able to observe the general background noise in the room and outside. On several occasions I could clearly hear talking outside in the street and children's voices. There is also a door slamming. I then asked him to reconstruct everything he could remember that happened during the recording. He recalled that his mother had told him afterwards that somebody had wanted to speak to his father, but on hearing that he was resting, had offered to come back. The mother then had told the person that she might as well speak to him there and then. It is therefore possible that she used the words which were recorded on the tape. The young man swears that he never heard his mother speak, nor does his mother remember having left the living room; but she must have gone out to let the visitor in. Strangely enough, this riddle was not solved as easily as it may appear. Because the young man has recorded some remarkable voices which bear every characteristic of the Voice Phenomenon, I was hesitant to say that this particular one was a freak pick-up. Besides, he was quite distressed about the fate of his grandmother when I met him. Later, I made three copies of this voice for my lecture at the S.A.G.B.; whether I accidentally amplified the original voice to the exact level or for some other reason, when I listened to the recording again, after the lecture, I heard distinct noises which I associate with two women conversing and the closing of a door afterwards.

This is, of course, a case where a voice printer could eliminate any doubt. Although experiments with a voice printer involve complicated laboratories and machines which are not easily accessible to everybody, all technological inventions are expensive in the development stage. To build the first Concorde supersonic aircraft, many millions had to be spent, and for years anybody who wanted to see this plane had to go to the place where she was built. A year or two from now, the Concorde will be a familiar sight on the runways of all international airports.

No doubt, within the foreseeable future, voice printers will be part of some recording machine which has been designed specially for electronic voices.

There is no foolproof method which prevents misinterpretation of voices. Common sense is the only yardstick we can apply. A person without common sense should not experiment; but I could easily carry this prohibition further: such a person should not be allowed to drive a car, or engage in most activities of the human race other than eating and sleeping, and I am certain that such a person would either over eat or poison himself in the process.

Gordon Turner's fear of danger, however, goes far deeper. He published a long article (Psychic News 15 May 71) under the title "Raudive Voices: references to Hitler are dangerous", in answer to an article by R. A. Cass (P.N.

the previous week). Turner draws attention to the kind of danger he had in mind, the 'neo-fascist undertone of some of the voices'. He had mentioned this point on *Late Night Line-Up,* but only as a passing comment and I had not paid much attention to it. This is how Gordon Turner sees the problem:

"Now for the "lower astral", "rescue circles" and "Hitler with his troops of bemused devotees." Fair enough, we know all about those who are so spiritually sick they create their own hell.

I have experience of circles which try to help such people—I believe I have considerably more experience than Cass. I acknowledge these facts, just as I realise slums, crime, drug-addiction, disease and prostitution exist in this world.

Precisely the same spiritual law pertains. Contact with troubled souls should be based on helpful service rather than excited dabbling. Having said this, I must repeat I have very real doubts as to the non-material source of these voices.

One paragraph in Cass' article should be quoted in full. It points to the reason why I believe "Breakthrough" should not have been published and is potentially more dangerous than selling ouija boards as toys:

"If there is a spirit world it is full of the flotsam and jetsam of our military and mercantile civilisation. If a door has been opened between this world and the next, then the masses armed with their cheap transistor sets and £5 Hong Kong tape recorders will participate in this new Hydesville despite Gordon Turner, the Pope and the Government."

Let us suppose for a moment that Cass is right. The Raudive voics stem from discarnate entities living in a lower astral hell any anyone can make contact with them with the aid of a cheap transistor and £5 tape recorder.

Does he really think it is safe for anyone and everyone

to open themselves to this type of influence? Has he the slightest conception of how dangerous this might be?

There is a direct link between fascism, black magic and contact with impersonating earthbound entities who deliberately delude and pervert others. Himmler received messages from just such a source.

He was told he was the reincarnation of Henry the Fowler and encouraged in his policy of exterminating the Jews. He believed it was possible to harness occult powers to help the Nazi war machine.

For this purpose a special circle of SS elite was formed. When working on a film screenplay recently, I interviewed a former member of this group who now lives in Hamburg.

At least three top Nazi leaders were at one time or another concerned with black magic. From information I have been able to gather, it seems possible that what Cass describes as "tyrant kingdoms in spirit realms holding sway over minds if not bodies" may well have been directly connected with the fascist insanity which swept Europe 40 years ago.

Are those the sort of doors that Cass wants opened with £5 Hong Kong tape recorders?

There is another real danger. Tape recorders are liable to outside interference. A case was reported recently of a woman who had a "talking" carpet sweeper! It was picking up radio signals.

Tape recorders have been known to pick up fragments of radio and TV broadcasts. Wishful thinking, a little imagination and a mixture of languages might cause an unbalanced person to believe these were outside communications and act on what he believes are spirit messages.

Cass is wrong. I have not spent most of my life "trying to prise open the doors of the spirit world." As a natural medium I found them open in my early childhood. I saw then, as I see now, a world of light and beauty.

I have devoted most of my life to trying to help others not to fear death and endeavouring to understand the supreme spirit plan and where I might best co-operate on its furtherance.

If the Raudive voices are stemming from a paranormal source, then I would regard some of the references to Hitler as significant and dangerous. There, we are told, Hitler is worshipped 20 hours a day.

There is already enough darkness and ignorance in this world. Does Cass really believe we want more?

He writes: "A parallel universe may be revealed with intelligences existing in a continuum where our moral and ethical standards have no frame of reference.

"Such a breakthrough will bring sweeping changes in our thinking. As with the release of atomic energy we shall be faced by a dramatic choice between good and evil."

Most of us, I believe, have already made that choice!"

There can be little doubt that the author is sincere in his opinion; all the same, I believe he is misguided because he takes the quotes about Hitler out of context and therefore distorts the true balance of presentation. He over-states his case, trying to crack a nut with the proverbial sledge hammer.

On 29 May, R. A. Cass replied in his article "Nearly everything today is dangerous". There is little I could add to Mr. Cass' competent answers to Turner's theories.

"Gordon Turner reveals confused, ambivalent and even contradictory attitudes. While striving to interpret them (the Voices) as some kind of electronic freak, he warns readers of the extreme danger of their promulgation.

His warnings that the book "Breakthrough" should never have been published and carries more potential danger than a ouija board are calculated to send the lethargic and indifferent scurrying to booksellers for a copy to see what all the fuss is about.

Any schoolboy knows that to talk about banning a book is to treble the demand for it! Suppression of facts is no solution in this case.

The publisher vainly tried, in the TV discussion, to get over to Turner and Rosalind Heywood that here was a phenomenon which had not yielded to the most searching examination of recording experts under laboratory conditions.

The "voices" were not random scraps of radio transmissions, but intelligible messages directed at specific persons and claiming to be from the "dead".

When Turner speaks of "talking carpet sweepers" and tape recorders picking up radio signals, he is referring to what is known as a dry joint in an electrical circuit, which acts as a rectifier or detector much as in the old crystal sets.

I have a small electronic device which, when held against a metal lampshade in one of my consulting rooms, picks up BBC 2. It should not do this, but it does occur in one room.

The exact point of contact with the lampshade is quite critical. This is, however not an occult phenomenon, merely BBC 2. It would require a fevered imagination to convert it to Raudive-type voices.

"Breakthrough" describes more persistent, complex phenomena, disturbing in some aspects, but no more so than some utterances in books produced through automatic writing.

But, says Turner, "if it is true, then it is dangerous." In addition, it is "dreary and boring." He regales us with the sinister outlines of a fascist conspiracy with undertones of black magic and the Nazis.

It is impossible here to go into the question of the involvement of the Nazi hierarchy with secret occult chiefs. As far back as 1941, H. G. Baynes, in a masterly work on the demoniac aspects of Nazism, ("Germany Possessed", Jonathan Cape) explored the whole of this territory. He should be read by every student of mediumship.

Contemporary authorities on Hitler and the Nazis, e.g. Alan Bullock, offer more mundane explanations. Millions of people were murdered in Eastern Europe during Hitler's years of power.

It should surprise no one if these doomed individuals are obsessed with the name Hitler in their fragmentary post-mortem communications.

Turner is concerned with slums, prostitution and drugs as causes of earthbound conditions in his "lower astral". I repeat we should look at the systematic torture endemic to the 20th century for the confusion in the Raudive communications.

Far from seeking neo-Nazis on our tape recorders, we should be working out ways and means of dealing with the even greater problems of hydrogen bombs, over-population and global pollution which, within 25 years if not remedied, will produce a mass exodus to Turner's "lower realms" and more terrified and confused astral entities, voicing "banalities".

I do not advocate dabbling with tape recorders any more than I would undirected ouija board experimentation. But if a chink has—accidentally of with intent—opened in the veil between this existence and another, then it will not be possible to close it by placing its source book on Turner's Index.

We are in any case passive participants in an electronic network via the mass media: McLuhan speaks of the "global village" and Teilhard de Chardin of his "Noosphere".

Even as Turner and I engage in this discussion, experimenters in other parts of the world are receiving tape recorded messages from the so-called dead (P.N. May 15, "Inaudible spirit voice taped").

This seems to vindicate those who for half a century have predicted spririt electronic communication. H. D. Thorp in his "Etheric Vision" (Rider) foresaw this development nearly 40 years ago.

Now about the dangers. If some misguided, unwary cleric in an obscure parish magazine fulminates about the dangers of Spiritualism, he soon has Maurice Barbanell on his neck and with good reason! Turner's "bogy man" theme should be subjected to the same critical scrutiny.

Practically everything we do nowadays is dangerous, fattening, or something. But we have to go on living anyway!

The trouble with the Raudive researches is that they originated outside the mainstream of Spiritualistic and psychic research tradition. They will continue, with or without the blessings of these bodies.

Charles Fort saw it all coming in the 1930's and looked for psychic intrusions occuring outside both the Spiritualist and orthodox scientific frame of reference."

I appreciate and respect Gordon Turner's concern but I do not share it. Spiritualists will have to come to terms with the Voice Phenomenon sooner or later; it cannot be banned or wished away. Even if Professor Bender's alternative theory should emerge as the true explanation of the voices, namely that the mediumship of the experimenter causes thought forms from the subconscious to manifest themselves as voices on the tape, it would be a challenge to every Spiritualist. On the whole, I believe that the shock of learning about the Voice Phenomenon has done the Spiritualist movement a great deal of good, even if it has only woken up many lethargic minds and shaken the conceited. This is perhaps the only criticism I have to make about Spiritualism: within its ranks I have met some members who are far more conceited and contemptuous of those who do not share their psychic gifts than the most arrogant and pompous scientist or professor. I have often been tempted to quote St. Paul to them: 'yet the greatest gift is Charity'.

8

The Church and the Voices

In June 1971, a series of articles appeared in English and
Irish newspapers which were obviously designed to bring
one issue into the open: the reaction of the churches to
the Voice Phenomenon. After the first *Late Late Show* in
Dublin in which a Roman Catholic priest from Rome had
participated, the writer said: "I was absolutely certain that
the next morning some public denunciation would be read
from all the pulpits in Dublin, signed by Archbishop John
Charles McQuaide; fellow journalists who were more
acquainted with the Dublin scene were equally sure that
no such denouncement would be made. They were right".
The journalist then gave his reasons for being suspicious
of the attitude the Church appeared to have adopted:
"In spite of the greater flexibility of the Church after
Vatican II, I found it difficult to accept that the Hierarchy
had turned its back on Cardinal Roberti and Mgr.
Palazzini, whose *Dictionary of Moral Theology* (1962)
reiterated the decrees of the Holy Office which categorically
prohibit any experiment '. . . irrespective of any theoretical
explanation of phenomena whether they are manifestations
of a preternatural order or belonging to the sphere of
natural laws.' There is no doubt that Raudive's experiments
fall within this category."
Later in the article, he analysed some aspects of my
presentation of the Voice Phenomenon which struck him to
be peculiar. By innuendo I was made out to be an *éminence*

grise who "with ease produced a Superior of the Pauline Fathers from Rome who endorsed everything Peter Bander said."

What exactly is the attitude of the Church? For a start, it is quite impossible to speak of 'the Church' because there happen to be some differences of opinion between the various denominations with regard to a great number of subjects. There are, in fact some very fundamental differences between their beliefs in life after death. A strictly Non-conformist Christian would have to overcome substantial difficulties if he wanted to subscribe to anything but the 'resurrection of the body' on the day of the 'Last Judgement'. Within the Anglican Church both the Non-conformist and the Catholic doctrines are represented. The Roman Catholic Church, on the other hand, teaches a more active life after death; Intercession by the Saints and 'passing through a period of purification' are two definite creeds of the faith. As far as the Jewish religion is concerned, it would be impossible to link the Voice Phenomenon with any belief in a post-mortal existence. There has been no 'Jewish reaction' to *Breakthrough* and only a remote 'non-conformist interest' was shown with warnings and quotations taken from passages of the Old Testament, suspecting the voices to be of the Devil and possibly an "Abomination to the Lord". Apart from Mgr. Pfleger, Prof. Frei (both Roman Catholics) and Dr. Voldemars A. Rolle, who is a Lutheran Pastor and a Professor of Physics, no churchmen had commented publicly on the voices before *Breakthrough* was published in Britain. I anticipated an active reaction in the English speaking world because there prevails a greater sense of individuality and less coercion of opinion among Ministers of Religion in Britain and America. The reaction of the Irish depended, in my opinion, entirely on the support from the Catholic Church, and, if at all possible, a spokesman who could speak with authority.

In order to gauge a general reaction on the religious scene, I consulted Douglas Brown, the Religious Correspondent of the BBC, whose predictions and forecasts about

Church elections, votes cast during synods and appointments to high offices have always been astonishingly accurate. He was confident there would be a large consensus of opinion in favour of the experiments from Anglican and Catholic churchmen; he predicted that *The Church Times* would strike a cautious note and give prominence to Catholic theologians being involved in the experiments, the Catholic papers would play the whole thing down, but there would be no shortage of bishops or priests of either Church to discuss the book and the voices on radio or television. Mr. Brown immediately arranged a discussion for his radio programme *Sunday,* but he only chose laymen to participate. He predictions were correct in every respect.

The Right Reverend Dr. Butler, Bishop of Connor, was the first leading Anglican churchman publicly to voice his opinion:

"I am definitely impressed and willing to be impressed by this phenomenon. The point is made by the author that this is an additional proof of life after death. The interesting thing is that the book is published at a time when a great many people have given up the idea of a life after death. I would welcome the book for this reason alone. But having said that, I feel very much in the position of a plain man's friend: I wonder if it will be of great help to ordinary people at this stage."

When, at the end of a fifteen minute television debate, Bishop Butler was asked to make a final comment on *Breakthrough,* he said:

"I think one of the truest remarks in the book, referring to the whole of the experiments, is that they are in their infancy. I think this is very true indeed; this is only the beginning."

This can be described as a classic 'Anglican statement': restrained non-committal and diplomatic. When commenting on what the voices were saying Bishop Butler's answer would have done credit to any diplomat commenting on a controversial issue: "My reaction would be as if I was making a rather badly connected transatlantic telephone call, and could not quite make out what the voice was." It was only when I watched the recorded programme that I realised the Bishop had skilfully avoided being drawn into committing himself.

The initial participation of Roman Catholic priests in the experiments and their contributions to Raudive's book were coincidental. One journalist researched into any possible links between the Church and the author; he wrote: "I discovered that Dr. Konstantin Raudive is completely unknown in Vatican circles. His only contact in Rome appears to be Dr. Sargenti, the Professor of Psychology at the University. However it stands to reason that some of the contributors to *Breakthrough* must have been well known in the Vatican." Professor Gebhard Frei was President of *Imago Mundi* and the Vatican's expert in parapsychology, and The Right Rev. Monsignor Pfleger, a Chaplain to the Holy See and Professor of Theology. The latter had already expressed his opinion in a high-powered Catholic magazine and his two articles were later condensed and reproduced in our book. The only direct approach to the Vatican in regard to *Breakthrough* was made unofficially when I asked Archbishop Cardinale for an opinion of Professor Frei. Mgr. Cardinale is the Apostolic Nuncio to Belgium, Luxembourg and the E.E.C. and regarded as the Vatican's senior diplomat in Western Europe. In order to obtain from him any comment whatever, he had to be put in the picture; he wanted to know why I needed the information and how I was going to use it if he got it for me. He stressed the point that no conclusions could possibly be drawn as to the validity of the Voice Phenomenon from any report or opinion of Professor Frei. It was not until six weeks after the publication of *Breakthrough* that Archbishop Cardinale mentioned the Voice Phenomenon to me again. In a letter he wrote to me: "I was greatly impressed by the book and I have, of course, spoken to many about the Phenomenon. Naturally, it is all very mysterious, but we know the voices are there for all to hear them." At no time has Archbishop Cardinale even hinted at the fact that Pope Paul VI and Vatican circles were acquainted with the Voice Phenomenon. Some journalists who later wrote about the attitude of the Church to the voices, have implied that I had some 'hot line' to the Vatican and therefore knew about Pope Paul bestowing the Commander's Cross of St. Gregory the Great upon the discoverer of the voices in 1969. During a programme I mentioned Archbishop Cardinale's reference to the voices, without giving his name and I refused to show the letter to a reporter afterwards. My refusal merited the following paragraph in his article: "Mr. Bander was quite adamant in refusing to give the names of eminent churchmen; he explained that he had to respect the wishes of these gentlemen not to publish private correspondence. Neither could he be persuaded to elaborate further on their attitudes."

Contrary to some reporters' speculations and wishful thinking, there has been no conspiracy; only perhaps a surprising number of coincidences and parallel developments. It was certainly news to me that Friedrich Jürgenson was created a Commander of the Order of St. Gregory the Great, and his close connection with the Pope and the Holy See for almost a decade was unknown to me until Mr. Jürgenson told me about it in the summer of 1971. Apparently an Italian journalist had mentioned these facts in April and a British colleague later fitted them into a pattern which, at first glance, seemed to substantiate the theory that I was 'covering up' for the Vatican and in return received assistance from Catholic spokesmen in television debates.

Another coincidence was that in 1970 I had written *The Prophecies of Malachy,* a lighthearted book about the future of the papacy. Although completely unrelated and irrelevant this was brought up more than once to suggest a link between me and the administration of the Catholic Church.

There has never been an official Catholic attitude to the Voice Phenomenon; the opinions expressed by some well informed and highly respected prelates and priests were their own. On the other hand, more Catholic priests have commented on and discussed the voices than ministers of other religious denominations. The difficulty, of course, is to find a suitable platform on which to conduct a serious dialogue. It is unreasonable to expect that such an important subject could be dealt with in fifteen minutes flat, giving about three minutes to each member of a panel after a five minute general introduction to the Phenomenon. Unfortunately, this is what has happened frequently on television and radio, with some notable exceptions: the *Late Night Line-Up* programme, which was allowed to over-run its allotted time considerably, BBC Radio Sheffield where Ian Masters gave an entire *Home Tonight* programme to the subject, and Telefis Eireann's *Late Late Show* which devoted two Saturday nights to the Voice Phenomenon. It was on the Irish television programmes that the religious implications of the voices were not only aired but examined in depth. Much of the religious discussion which followed was in direct response to the *Late Late Shows* of RTE.

Because all the different aspects of the Voice Phenomenon were discussed on these programmes, it will be necessary to come back to the *Late Late Show* for assessment and evaluation of their achievements; The comments by Fr. Pistone and the subsequent dialogue must therefore be seen in the context of the whole programme. On 8 and 22 May 1971, Fr. Pistone spoke as one of the two main contributors to the Shows. His position has been described by different newspapers and magazines as 'the representative of the Vatican' (Quarterly Review of the Churches' Fellowship), 'Superior General of the Paulist Fathers' (in an RTE announcement and five newspapers), and it has always been inferred that his comments carried the official seal of approval by the Vatican. Father Pistone was, in fact, Superior of the Society of St. Paul in England, deputising for the Regional Superior, Father Valente, who was in Rome at the time of the broadcasts. The Society of St. Paul is a Catholic Order charged with teaching, and acts through

93

Press, Radio and Television. They control most of the Catholic Church's radio and television stations, especially in the Far East; they publish one of the largest colour magazines in the world, and they have printing presses, publishing houses and news services all over the world. Most of their Superiors are Italians and Rome-trained. Among the priests and brothers are leading theologians as well as excellent craftsmen, printers, broadcasters and professional men of various descriptions and talents. Father Pistone made it quite clear at the outset of his deliberations that he could only speak for himself and endeavour to explain in simple terms what he believed to be the attitude of the Catholic Church. The first question Fr. Pistone answered concerned this attitude of the Church to the voices in general.

"Is there anything in these experiments, in the voices or in the book that might be said to be against Catholic teaching or theology?" Gay Byrne asked.

"I have read the book from cover to cover. I accept everything in it as a scientific experiment. The subtitle itself states that it is 'an amazing experiment'. I do not see anything against the teaching of the Church; if anything, the book confirms the teaching of the Church and what we believe, namely that there is life after death. It confirms no more than that, there is life after death; there is a contact we can have with people who have died. This contact, so the Church maintains, is the help we can give them. It also becomes clear from the content of many of the voices that they cannot help themselves."

Father Pistone was then asked whether he believed what and who the voices purported to be.

"I believe that these voices are something extraordinary. I could not point my finger at any one of them and say 'This is definitely such and such a person'. The message these voices hold for me is confirmation—if such confirmation were necessary—that there is life after death. There is a stage in the life after death during which one is in expectation of fulfilling one's own life term, so that we ultimately can return to our Creator and be happy for ever."

Thirdly the question was raised of the dangers inherent in enquiring into life after death and the possible intervention by evil spirits.

" I do not see any danger whatever, neither do I see any reason for fear. Besides, scientifically it has yet to be established that we are really dealing with voices from the dead. What we are faced with is a phenomenon; we need accept no more and can accept no less. Personally, I am satisfied that there is life after death and I also believe that there is a contact between the living and the dead because this contact is part of the Church's concept; the Communion of Saints, if you like. We can always contact the departed through our prayers and help them. Therefore, if they can contact us, directly or indirectly, it is a matter which is under the power of God because the departed are under His power also. As to the question of evil, everything should be seen and done in the proper way and manner. Naturally, there could be maniacs in the field of the Voice Phenomenon because evil use and abuse applies to every experiment and invention. Take the telephone, for example; this too can be abused. However, if experiments and inventions are conducted or treated in the proper manner, they yield scientific research. Such a research need not necessarily be conducted to gain advantage. In most of us curiosity is an inherent quality. We just want to learn and to know more; that is the only aim. But, as I said, everything can be abused."

Father Pistone's statements are clear and to the point. There is no diplomatic ambiguity in them, nor any attempt to avoid the issues. Needless to say, what he has said on the television made the news. The religious implications were suddenly given priority. Dr. Brendan McGann, the Director of the Institute of Psychology, Dublin, and Professor of Psychology at TCD, while stating that he had apparently succeeded in reproducing the Phenomenon, said in *The Irish Times* (9 July 1971): "It is unfortunate that the researcher and some of his collaborators identified the form of existence intimated by the voices as that of the theological after-life. It was even suggested that the voice entities were speaking from a state of existence known to Catholics as Purgatory. If the Voice Phenomenon is proven to be an authentic one, it appears highly unlikely that this could be so, but rather that the voices are evinced by an aspect of normal existence which has been unknown hitherto."

On 15 July 1971, *The Irish Times* carried an interview with Father Pistone in which Jan van Duren raised those questions which may have been in the minds of many people: did Father Pistone regret having appeared on television in such a controversial matter, and did he really feel justified in explaining the attitude of the Church to the Voice Phenomenon in the way he had done? This interview, which has also appeared in English newspapers and magazines, is probably the most important document available today when we talk of an 'official Catholic viewpoint'. It is worthwhile reading in its entirety because the questions asked are as important as the answers.

A month ago you appeared on the Late Late Show *of* Telefís Eireann *for the second time within two weeks, discussing the book* Breakthrough, *the Voice Phenomena and the extraordinary claims made by scientists that they are communicating with the dead. Has there been any repercussion or reaction to your participation?*

From what I have heard, there appears to have been a great interest in this subject, especially in Ireland. Of course, I cannot evaluate my own presence on the programmes because I don't know whether my participation made all that difference; the fact that I am a Catholic priest may, of course, have been viewed with some apprehension by some.

Do you believe, on reflection, that a representative of the Catholic Church should have participated in such a scientific dialogue, which, after all, touched on a very delicate subject, namely that of dead people actually getting in touch with the living?

I believe that this was very important and necessary. First, I had the opportunity of reaching far more people via this medium than I could possibly in a lifetime of preaching. Secondly, although these discussions were mainly about scientific problems, a priest will always bring to such a discussion the moral and theological points of view; this is important, especially in a predominantly Catholic country. Morals and theology play a very important part in all questions concerning psychology, parapsychology and similar disciplines which deal with the human mind. It was, as it turned out, quite unimportant that I am not an electronics expert; there were quite a number of reputable scientists present, whose word I am quite happy to take as far as the scientific facts go. I feel very strongly on the question of the Church participating in all questions which directly or indirectly concern Her faithful.

Until very recently the Church has either kept quiet or treated such subjects with contempt. What has brought about the change in the Church's attitude?

I don't think the Church has ever kept quiet! Within the Church, many eminent individuals have always kept the dialogue going. This applies to many subjects. The Church has Her own experts on all subjects. It is the task of the advisers that nothing should be attributed to the Church's teaching that might be contrary to the authority given to Her by Christ. However, the attitude of the Church to many subjects has become more flexible—it has not changed on matters of principle—since the last Vatican Council.

It is true to say that the programmes on which you appeared went far beyond the usual platitudes. Life after death was discussed outside the usual framework of Heaven and Hell, or Purgatory for those who qualify for neither. In the eyes of many viewers, the programme was revolutionary.

We have always believed and taught that there is life

97

after death. There has never been a formula in which the Church could present the existence of an after-life in black and white terms. A discussion on a scientific experiment such as the Voice Phenomenon could make a few things clearer. But it would never produce a full answer to many questions. The Church wants far more than just voices. Let us assume that the scientists will come up with irrefutable proof that these voices really come from the dead; that would still not solve any problem with which the Church is concerned. Neither do I think that it would make dying more palatable to people. One member of the audience was very concerned with the actual resting place of the souls. The Church teaches that we leave our physical body behind and receive a spiritual body. But we must get away from the terminology, so often used, which implies floating about, flying with wings or physical confinement in one place or other, such as Heaven or Hell. Yet, the moment you stop using these terms of reference, you are likely to talk above the head of many people. This is what I meant when I said that the Church has never really been able to present this subject just in black and white.

One of the questions you answered on the programme concerned the actual content of many of the recorded messages; it was suggested that they were banal or pathetic. Does this worry you or put you off?

Many of the voices ask for our prayers. This is, of course, in accordance with our own teaching. The Church has always maintained that the dead need our prayers. It makes no difference that these voices ask for prayers: the Church has always offered them for the departed. However, this raises a very important point: in the past, the Catholic Church has always been very firm on the question of Spiritualism. Much criticism has been levelled against the firm stand we have taken and, on Her part, the Church has always condemned this practice. This is a very complex problem, and I do not feel qualified to pronounce on the Church's reason at length. However, I go as far as to say that the contents of many of the purported messages are contrary to the teaching of the Church. So far, the Church had never to verify the testimony of anybody who had died. When it comes to verifying and investigating the claims of people who purport to have heard voices or seen visions, you are dealing with a very delicate subject, to say the least. You must ascertain that you are not dealing with a person's imagination or, as the evidence in the past has shown, very often with a mental illness. This is the reason why the Church moves so very slowly when investigating such claims. In fact, before the Church is prepared to accept that there were voices or a vision, irrefutable proof of a divine intervention must be there for all to see.

But why has the Church always condemned Spiritualism without ever investigating some of the remarkable demonstrations of genuine phenomena?

Who says that they are really genuine? Perhaps they are, perhaps they are not. What proof has there been? Yet, there have been so many contradictory and disturbing reports in the past, throwing a light on certain Spiritualistic practices, that it was and has been right to express serious doubt about the value of Spiritualism. The Church disapproves, and I say this in all humility, of the claim some Spiritualists put forward, that certain Saints, such as St. Paul, the patron of my own Order, comes to their seances and teaches them things which are totally stupid and contrary to everything St. Paul has said in his letters. There is a simple answer for those people. Let them look up the gospel of St. Luke and read in Chapter 16 what Christ has to say about such things. Verse 31 should provide the reason why the Church also disapproves of the practice of calling up dead persons. We believe it to be wrong to disturb their peace just because we feel like it.

In how far are the experiments described in Break-

through *and those experiments discussed on television, different, and what part does or should the Church play in the development of such experiments?*
The activity, the initiative, if you like, throughout these experiments appears to be on the part of—well, let us just say "them", whoever they are. But, let us get one thing straight. We are putting the cart before the horse; we are discussing this on the assumption that we are dealing with the voices of the dead. If this hypothesis is right, then it looks very much as if they are anxious to communicate. Why this is so I don't know, nobody knows as yet. But there is another difference: these voices are physically there and can be proven to be there by all sorts of mehanical and electronic gadgets. We also know from experts that these voices were not produced by human agencies nor any means known to the world of physics or electronics. We cannot get away from the physical reality of the voices. Hence the experiments are justified, they are credible, but we cannot understand them. Nor do we know the purpose behind the communications.
As to the role of the Church in further developments, I am sure that the Church will and must keep a close check on that which is happening in this field. Had this just been an experiment of one man or a small group of people, no doubt the Church would leave the whole matter strictly alone; however, these experiments have been widely publicised and made a wide impact. Ordinary people may be persuaded to carry out experiments which are not conducted under scientific supervision; the Church must be prepared to speak with authority on this subject.
So far, the Church has found no reason to be against experiments with Voice Phenomena; the Church has no reason to say that they are wrong. Neither has it any reason to say that they are right and should be advocated. I doubt whether the Church will ever make an official pronouncement on the matter. Let me briefly

Throughout the controlled experiment Dr. Raudive was completely isolated from the machines and control devices set up by the Pye Engineers. Ronald Maxwell (Sunday Mirror) was in charge of the proceedings, and twelve observers were present at any one time during the experiment. (l. to r.): Victor Bearman, Churches' Fellowship for Psychical Research, David Stanley, Ronald Maxwell, Dr. Raudive, and Peter Bander.

The Right Reverend Mgr. Stephen O'Connor, Vicar General and Principal Roman Catholic Chaplain to the Royal Navy (right) listening to the playback of a recording on which a voice had manifested itself purporting to be that of a young naval officer who had committed suicide two years earlier. Dr. Raudive (left) had recorded the voice at an earlier session.

The Rev. Prof. Dr. Gebhard Frei, "All that I have read and heard forces me to believe that the voices come from transcendental, individual entities. Whether it suits me or not, I have no right to doubt the reality of the voices."

The Rev. Fr. Pistone, S.S.P.: "I do not see anything against the teaching of the Catholic Church in the Voices, they are something extra-ordinary but there is no reason to fear them, nor can I see any danger."

Maurice Barbanell, Editor Psychic News: "The future lies with instruments capable of recording vibrations or radiations emanating from the spirit world which are not normally receptive to man's five senses."

The Right Rev. Dr. Butler, Anglican Bishop of Connor: " I am definitely impressed and willing to be impressed by this phenomenon. As to the whole of the experiments, this is after all, only the beginning."

The Rt. Rev. Mgr. Prof. C. Pfleger: "Facts have made us realise that between death and resurrection there is yet another realm of post-mortal existence. Christian theology has little to say about this realm."

His Excellency, Archbishop H. E. Cardinale, Apostolic Nuncio to Belgium, Luxembourg and the E.E.C.: "Naturally it is all very mysterious, but we know the voices are there for all to hear them."

Friedrich Jürgenson discovered the Voice Phenomenon in 1959. His main aim has been to build a bridge between the two worlds which seemed to be so near and yet so far.

In 1969 Mr. Jürgenson was created a Knight Commander of the Order of St. Gregory the Great by Pope Paul VI. There has never been an *official* opinion expressed by the Vatican with regard to the voices, however, since the last Vatican Council, the attitude of the Church towards research in this field has been most encouraging.

"Does Rufus hold the secret of the Voices of the Dead?" was the headline in one of the newspaper articles. The acute hearing of the four year old Great Dane seemed to enable him to perceive sounds immediately, long before the experimenters did.

The voice prints (below) were made by the Central Office for Telegraphic Communication, Berlin, and show the voice of Jürgenson (top) starting an experiment and a "spirit" voice (below).

From a purely physical point of view, it appears quite possible that Rufus would hear many of the sounds which are practically inaudible to the human ear.

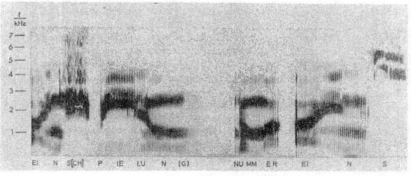

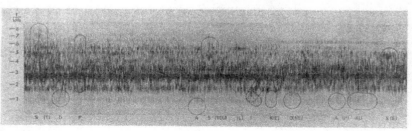

come back to a point which was raised earlier: I questioned the sanity of those who maintain that St. Paul and other Saints were giving them new teachings. The Church teaches that the Divine revelation is complete. The last book in the New Testament is the final chapter of the Divine revelation. The Church has the authority—given to Her by Christ—to teach Her faithful and instruct according to the Divine revelation. Christ would not have said so, had He intended to send latter-day prophets down to us who would change the Divine revelation. The Voice Phenomena, on the other hand, neither teach nor attempt to change anything that the Christian Church has taught since the time of Christ; they make statements, they ask for prayers, they express in some cases happiness, in others, desperation and regret. The Church has always believed that life on this earth is followed by a period of purification. It matters little whether you call this purgatory or something else. It would therefore be conceivable that the contents of the voices which have been recorded fall within the concept of such a period; but I stress that this has yet to be proved.

But is it not conceivable that departed members of the Church might wish to add to the teaching? Who is to say that mediums who claim to have received teachings or instructions from certain Saints or Masters, are fakes or frauds?

I am not saying that they are fakes or frauds nor am I suggesting that what they received is purely imagination. What I am saying is that the Divine revelation is complete and that those whose books and letters have been added to the Divine revelation in the Gospels, would not change their teaching in such a pathetic way. The Spiritualists have no proof that it really is St. Paul or whoever claims to be talking to them. They may have convinced themselves that they heard a certain person but that is all. As far as the voices are concerned, that is, those which have been recorded, apart from the content, they are produced for everybody to hear and to examine. The danger of personal influence is removed. Mr. Peter Bander said on the programme that the only regret he had was about the gramophone record which was produced with the book. It gave an explanation of those voices; he felt that this might influence people to believe that they were actually hearing what the commentator said. He is absolutely right. The moment you subject a person to persuasion, you cannot be sure of objectivity. A medium, however honest as a person, would have no means of finding out who the purported message came from—if there really has been a message. Neither can we say that a voice on the tape recorder comes definitely from a certain person. The difference is that the medium will stake his or her reputation and integrity on such messages they give to people, whereas the Voice Phenomenon can be judged on its own merit without discrediting anybody.

Do you think that the Catholic Church will ultimately use a tape recorder when investigating purported apparitions? Do you believe that this would be a preferable method to that of the cumbersome process used at present?

The Church has Her own well tried methods and means of proving and disproving any claims. I don't think that we shall ever use any other method because why should we change something that has been both satisfactory and successful for something which would add nothing to the actual investigation in process? Whether or not a voice would come through whilst such an investigation is going on, could have no bearing on the case. Take, for example, the long and tedious process of canonisation: the person in question would have to perform the required miracles which are attributable to him, and these miracles must be proven. The Church is never concerned with verbal evidence but practical and tangible evidence which leaves no doubt whatever.

If you see no practical use for the Voice Phenomena in the Church, why then has She given the experiments Her support and allowed priests and even prelates to participate?

The Church realises that she cannot control the evolution of science. Here we are dealing with a scientific phenomenon; this is progress and the Church is progressive. I am happy to see that representatives of most Churches have adopted the same attitude as we have: we recognise that the subject of the Voice Phenomena stirs the imagination even of those who have always maintained that there could never be any proof or basis for discussion on the question of life after death. This book and the subsequent experiments raise serious doubts, even in the minds of atheists. This alone is a good reason for the Church supporting the experiments. A second reason may be found in the greater flexibility of the Church since Vatican II, we are willing to keep an open mind on all matters which do not contradict Christ's teaching.

On his return from the General Council in Rome, the former Regional Superior of the Society of St. Paul, The Very Rev. Don Valente, a Doctor of Theology, discussed Fr. Pistone's opinions with a small group of friends, all of whom had read the book and the account of Fr. Pistone's interview.

He was not so much concerned with the voices but with the 'period of purification' or Purgatory. As Fr. Valente is no longer Regional or local Superior, he stressed that he could only give a personal opinion and explain his own beliefs: "As I see this matter, I cannot subscribe to the term 'scientific' which has been attributed to the voices; we really know nothing outside our five senses. Those concerned should not apply their research results to Christianity just because they are Christians. It has been said that there is a period of purification after death and it has been assumed that we spent months or years in Purgatory. I believe that we meet Christ at the very moment of our death. Once you approach Christ, he purifies you immediately, in a second, if you like! I believe that the masses we say and the use of holy water for the purification of the departed souls are only pious thoughts and good intentions. God does not need our prayers; God is justice and can take care of matters without our prayers which we say at given times. All prayers go into a spiritual bank account towards the meeting with Christ. As far as the experiments with the voices are concerned, I noticed that most of the experimenters are Christians and therefore apply their approach to their Christian way of thinking. Hence you have 'Christian experiments'. Had these experiments been carried out elsewhere, say in a Buddhist country or among Muslims, the results would have been given a different slant. Nobody knows what life after death is like. How much is our own mind dissociated from or connected with our former existence? I base my opinion on the teaching of St. Paul to the Corinthians. We have already reached salvation on the cross at Calvary. Once we are dead, we are with Christ; there is no need or desire to communicate with the living on earth, and Purgatory has no place or time factor. Therefore the voices cannot come from Purgatory."

His view is similar to the theories put forward by Professor McGann. I do not know how widely held Fr. Valente's ideas are within the Catholic Church. Since the Second Vatican Council, Catholic theologians of different persuasions are free to voice their opinions publicly. It is interesting that even within the same religious Order strongly contrasting views can be held and expressed.

However, the one question which has yet to be answered 'officially' or unofficially by the theologians, appeared in a letter to *The Irish Times:*

"If these be the dead, and if it be indeed a sin to listen to them, is there any way, short of a couple of decades of the Rosary, of inducing them to get to Hell off the air?"

9

Late Late Breakthrough

After the first *Late Late Show*, one journalist wrote: "What made this show so unique was that until last night the questions of life after death has never been publicly discussed in Ireland other than in the usual terms of Heaven and Hell, with Purgatory as an optional extra for those who qualified for neither."

This witty and perhaps cynical observation is nevertheless true to a large degree. I remember Gay Byrne saying to Pan Collins, just before the show started: "Here we go Pan. Let us hope we are doing the right thing. I'll bet we won't get much sleep tonight, just answering the telephones." Gay was absolutely right, all lines to the RTE studios were jammed with calls from viewers until the early hours of Sunday morning during and after both shows. The first evening on 8 May, took an unexpected turn; although a panel of experts had been given the book to read in advance, and were obviously expected to put forward critical arguments against the Voice Phenomenon, I realised soon that I received only support from the panelists. Ted Bonner, a well known television personality, an experienced panelist and, relevant to this programme, an electronics expert associated with Decca, was the first member of the panel to be invited to speak.

"I have spent most of my time last week reading the book right through. It would seem to me that it is quite scientifically proved—or at least the problem of the scientific research to which this all has been subjected—and it seems very very difficult to overcome. This is no trick and this is no gimmickry; this is something we have never dreamed of before." Mr. Bonner then gave some examples which had struck him as particularly significant and continued: "If somebody had enough brains to think up a remarkably clever trick with these voices, and scientists have done checks in a Faraday cage where the tape is isolated, and carefully sealed, well, if somebody is clever enough to do this, then he would certainly be clever enough to produce more cogent things on the tape itself. In conclusion on this point, I just want to say that it looks as though a door has just been slightly opened."

Miss Terry Prone, another member of the panel, simply asked whether these voices could not be 'left-overs' of conversations conducted many years ago and accidentally picked up, and she accepted my brief answer that this was highly unlikely. If there were fragments of speech floating around in the universe, surely we could not produce them on call-up. Gay Byrne remained completely unbiased throughout the programme. He asked the questions, and for the greater part, I was asked to answer them. Much of the time was taken up with technical explanations how to obtain voices. Father Pistone explained the religious implications and, before we had realised it, the time had run out.

Although immediately after the show we discussed the possibility of a second programme on the voices, it was about two hours later, when the telephone lines to the studio were still jammed and newspaper reporters wanted to know if Gay was definitely going to bring the subject back, that he suggested 22 May for a further debate on television. I left London for Belfast on 21 May because I had agreed to record two programmes for Ulster television. Two days earlier I received a small package from Pan Collins. It contained a small tape casette and a letter. Mrs. Collins told me that she had used a small portable tape recorder for the experiment. She and several of her friends were certain that there were voices on the tape and that she had used a diode for the recording. This instrument had been built for her by the sound technicians at RTE. Leslie Hayward and I listened to the tape twice. There were five or six distinct voices but we did not understand them clearly. Because I had very little time to listen any further, I suggested that we should make a copy, and thereby amplify the small tape onto a normal tape at a speed of $7\frac{1}{2}$ rpm. On the evening of 20 May, we played the tape once on my Ferguson tape recorder, using stereophonic earphones. Two of the voices were quite clear and audible. The first one we thought said "Frances" and the second voice said, very rapidly and in staccato fashion: "Your mother, Gay, your mother." I telephoned immediately to Dublin and asked Mrs. Collins if either sentence made any sense. It was on that evening when I heard for the first time that Mrs. Collins' Christian name is Frances. I had always believed it to be Pamela; I even used to call her Pam. Anyhow, I certainly had not associated Frances with Pan. She also told me that Gay Byrne's mother was dead. When I arrived at the studio of RTE on Saturday evening at 9 o'clock, I gave Pan Collins her tape; she suggested that I should put the copy of the tape on the studio's tape recorder in the monitor room, and she asked all the technicians and Gay Byrne to come too and listen. The sound engineers connected three loudspeakers and we played the tape. With other monitors going at full blast in the room next door, the playback conditions were far from ideal; yet in spite of the noise Mrs. Collins, three technicians, the engineer, Leslie Hayward and myself heard quite clearly: "Your mother, Gay, your mother." Gay Byrne was the only person in the room who said he honestly could not hear it. I believed Gay Byrne; the fact that seven out of eight people said they heard the sentence was in itself very unusual. I can only vouch for myself. I heard it even more clearly than the night before. Because of my own earlier experiences, when a voice purported to be that of my mother, I felt great sympathy with Gay; there is nothing more disconcerting and unnerving than to listen for the first time to such an experiment and hear one's mother. The emotional stress, combined with the tension which anyhow prevails during playback, tend to create resentment and even hostility. This was the first and only occasion when I noticed anger and coldness in Gay's facial expression. In fact, he reacted exactly as I had done, back in 1969. I spoke to Gay immediately afterwards and suggested that the contents of this incident should not be mentioned during the show which was about to start.

Apart from Father Pistone, Telefis Eireann had invited Ken Attwood, the chief engineer of Pye recordings, who had been in charge of the controlled experiment for *The Sunday Mirror*. I started the discussion, mentioning some of the viewers' letters I had received. Next came Ted Bonner who was asked if he had changed his mind since the last show. He had not; on the contrary, he had tried to find some reference in the Bible and came across a remarkable passage in Isaiah and he quoted:

"Men will say to you 'Seek the guidance of ghosts and familiar spirits who squeak and jibber.' A nation will surely seek guidance of its gods, of the dead on behalf of the living for an oracle or a message. They will surely say to you some such thing as this. But what they say is futile."

Miss Prone's reaction was a little unexpected: "Last time I came to the programme not believing actually and now I do not believe at all. I read the book pre-disposed to believe for all the wrong reasons. Peter is a professor, so he is a very good talker; he is trustworthy and believes in this phenomenon, so does Father Pistone. Dr. Raudive is a professor too. I think these are the wrong reasons."

When asked by Gay Byrne to explain what she thought the voices were and where they might come from she told the audience: "I have not got a fully reasoned antithesis to fit the pieces but what I have got is a reasonable doubt on many things. I do feel that it is far more likely these voices are left-overs."

"Do you mean that these voices are floating around in the air for thousands of years?" asked Gay Byrne.

"Yes, but they are not sound waves, they are not made by the human larynx, they are some sort of . . . . well I think it is very unlikely that it is done by the subconscious."

There followed a discussion between Ted Bonner, myself and Gay, all agreeing that Terry's suggestion was a little unreasonable. "We have now, if I may say so, skirted round the whole thing and are right back to the Sherlock Holmes dogma when he says to Watson: 'When you have satisfied every possibility, that which remains, however absurd, must be the answer,' " concluded Ted Bonner, "I do not agree that the voices are coming from the subconscious, neither do I believe for a moment that you can take electro-magnetic forces on a tape recorded from the subconscious. I believe this is the same sort of thing that we have been getting for years in seances where a medium is in touch with somebody on the other side . . . ."

Earlier in the afternoon I had a brief conversation with Ken Attwood. He had told me of his research during the last month, and especially his attempt to break the mystery of the voices. Without wishing to go into the reasons for the intensive research which had been carried out with Pye, who had originally been asked by *The Sunday Mirror* to conduct the controlled experiment, the report of which was rejected by the paper's editor-in-chief, Mr. Attwood assured me that everything had been done in their power to break the mystery. The actual dialogue between Gay Byrne and Ken Attwood is, in my opinion, important enough to be given as it took place:

Byrne: "I do not want to get into a long half-hour involvement about Faraday cages, diodes, or transistors and so on. Ken, in very simple language and very shortly, have you been able to break this thing technically?"

Attwood: "Technically, no. We have tried very hard. I personally have tried very hard; we have conducted a lot of experiments at work and we cannot break

H

this!"

Byrne: "Have you any explanation as a technical expert?"

Attwood: Quite frankly, no! I believe in it, I believe that there is something there . . . ."

Byrne: "You believe that it is what it purports to be?"

Attwood: "Let me explain to you that until two months ago I had no knowledge or idea about this whole thing. I was approached and I went along. I was quite sceptical and I must be frank about this."

At this point I interrupted Gay Byrne who was about to ask another question:

"You were not approached by us, Ken!"

Attwood: "Quite right, not by you, but by a newspaper in London."

Byrne: "Yes, Peter, this is important."

Attwood: "As I said, I went along and I got very interested. I have since then been following this thing through."

Byrne: "And you have tried to break this mystery in all technical terms?"

Attwood: "Yes!"

The discussion moved now into more technical details, oscillogram readings, video-tapes and voice printers. I mentioned that we only understood about five per cent of the audible voices and continued: "For example, before the show we tried upstairs an experiment. The tape was recorded by the researcher of this programme here in the studio."

I had no intention of actually discussing the contents of that experiment, nor, in fact of going into the matter further. I simply wanted to emphasise that out of a multitude of audible voices only a very small percentage could be understood by some of the listeners.

It was at this point that Gay Byrne interrupted me and explained to the audience: "Pan Collins tried to record something last week on her own tape recorder just to see what happens. These tapes were sent to Peter. Now, he swears and she swears, and we listened to it upstairs before the show . . . ."

Again I interrupted Gay: "And your technicians swear as well, Gay."

Gay Byrne continued: "Quite right, two of our technicians as well, who were upstairs, swear that they can hear what purports to be the voice of my mother addressing me, saying 'Your mother, Gay, your mother'. I have listened to it for about ten minutes so far, but not in the best of conditions, up there before the show. I can hear nothing except the hissing, but that is what they say."

Here a strange interruption came from somewhere above us. "I heard it too"—the voice came from one of the sound technicians, operating the large gallow-microphone above the audience in the studio.

"Who heard it?—You Dennis?—You are quite convinced you heard this?"

Dennis: "Yes, certainly yes."

Byrne: "Loud and clear?"

Dennis: "Of course not loud and clear but distinctly."

Byrne: "And you are quite convinced that it is a woman's voice saying 'Your mother, Gay, Your mother'?"

Dennis: "Yes, that is what I heard."

I felt very sorry for Gay Byrne; I still think that this dramatic scene was the wrong way of introducing him to the Voice Phenomenon. Earlier on, I mentioned Mr. Byrne's superb professionalism in compering the programme; the manner in which he handled this situation commanded my respect. After the programme, I wanted to apologise and let him know I regretted that this incident had been mentioned at all. "No, Peter," he said, "don't apologise; before you even spoke of an experiment, I knew that I would have to bring the matter up. Fair is fair, and that is what happened. My audience has a right to learn the whole truth, not only what is convenient or acceptable to the compere."

There were two more interruptions during the programme. Twice the Floor Manager stopped the show, each time informing Gay that all the telephone lines were jammed with calls from viewers. Hundreds of them had already left their questions with the switchboard, hundreds more wanted to get through and ask personal questions, but mainly they concerned technical aspects of how to obtain voices on their own tape recorders.

It was well after midnight when Gay Byrne signed off the air. It was past four o'clock Sunday morning when I returned to my hotel, only to find that the switchboard there was jammed with callers who had somehow discovered where I was staying for the night.

There is an epilogue to the two *Late Late Shows* in Dublin. A group of serious researchers got together. Mrs. Pan Collins and some of RTE's sound technicians were joined by Mr. Peter Prescott, Professor McGann, Mr. Ted Bonner and others. They have conducted most encouraging experiments over the last few months.

During the last week of January '72 I had the opportunity of joining one of the experiments carried out in Dublin. Fergus Graham (RTE sound engineer) had built a screening device for his diode similar to that used during the experiment with the Pye engineers. With assistance from Charles Byrne (RTE) a series of tests were carried out at the home of Mrs. Collins between 11 p.m. and 4 a.m. on Wednesday night. Although the voices which manifested themselves were of modest quality, I soon realised that the only person present for whom the messages were intended was Peter Prescott. A man's voice gave the name *Sam,* which, we were told was the name of Mr. Prescott's grandfather. Unfortunately, no earphones were available and we had to listen to one separate loudspeaker which had been connected to the tape recorder; as the treble and bass speakers were about ten inches apart from each other within the same casing, it proved at times extremely difficult to position the cabinet in such a way that we could all hear the voices at the same time. Nevertheless, we all heard them but their quality was too poor for us to receive any important message from them. Basically, the test was carried out to prove that voices might manifest themselves *in spite* of the screening device; from this point of view the experiment was successful.

Peter Prescott, B.A. (Mod.), a science philosopher of Trinity College, Dublin, has made a serious study of the Voice Phenomenon since June 1971. Although quite independently formulated, many of the points he made are identical with those expressed by Michael Kaye (see Chapter 11).

After Wednesday's experiment I discussed with him the degree of his success in recording Voice Phenomena.

"All experiments carried out in Dublin have yielded some degree of success" Mr. Prescott explained; "the best of the recordings were made on a rather cheap commercial tape recorder; however, in order to gain a better play-back quality, the tape was later copied onto another one, slightly amplifying the voices. It was quite remarkable that one voice clearly called out 'Gay'."

Peter Prescott's approach to the Voice Phenomenon is, of course, strongly influenced by his scientific work and studies at T.C.D. and the philosophical appraisal of the developments in Physics since Newton, contained in his thesis 'Models old and new', has helped him to formulate the kernel of a theory on the Voice Phenomena. "It suggests that the Voice Phenomena can only be acceptable to our present day science if we are prepared to extend our normal conception of reality by the addition of a new dimension. I do not think that this presents a problem because, for example, we have extended today the Newtonian type of mathematics by adding more dimensions as postulates, from which valid deductions can be made (with respect to contemporary physics).

"It therefore follows that any statement made about the Voice Phenomena has as much significance as any other statement derived from normal empirical evidence. It also follows that the precise nature of this new dimension does not have to be specifically defined in advance, for the purpose of the Voice Phenomena investigation.

"I have given much thought to the nature of the Voices and how they come to be. I believe their nature is similar to the type of experience we have when we are extremely tired, and when we have for one reason or another refused to go to sleep. Within our brain emerges an almost schizoid personality. We tend to perceive information from apparently nowhere, without our willing it. The most obscure and abstract thoughts manifest themselves under these circumstances. We have some long records of such experiences written down by medieval monks, for example. This information can be quite concrete; we tend to receive short phrases of information and appear to gain insights into and to contact an area of experience we are not normally aware of. The kind of sayings we accumulate in these moments tend to make little sense if written down. This area, I believe, is very similar to that of the voices. A great deal of the content of the voices is not really logical in our normal sense of the word. What we receive does not string together in long sentences which, for example, would give us predictable events. The Voices do not tell us what to do; they don't talk about an event tomorrow at twelve o'clock; they often mention something which to all intents and purposes is obscure, but it may to some degree contain an insight. So does the information I referred to earlier. We have therefore two areas of experience, one of them perceptible through the medium of the tape recorder, the other perceptible through our own mind. There is somewhere a connection between the two; I do not believe that these voices will change our notion of another type of existence; it will probably be shown that this 'after existence' is of a far more complex nature than we have preferred to imagine until now. We will undoubtedly suffer change due to this new notion of an 'after existence' and it will become a *public* notion, but at the moment I doubt whether it will change the present public notion of life after death.

"By our present standards of logic it is even possible to say that the nature of the voices shows an experience of a mental disorder, but this is not so. This is simply an area of existence about which we have little or no knowledge at all. We cannot use our normal pattern of logic because it is not based on that type of evidence. The evidence obtained from the voices is not imperical today, but it may become empirical in the future. The tape recorder has forced our hand and made it necessary to accept the voices as empirical evidence. However, as yet this evidence is only acceptable to a small number of people. I cannot really comment on the physical production of the Phenomenon but I do not believe that it is produced by the individual conscious or subconscious mind. I do not accept that the voices are 'extra terrestrial' in the normal geographical sense; it appears that the voices are within our environment and it often looks as if they hear, see or sense features of our own environment which we recognise and they comment upon. This leads me to the conclusion that they are during the time of transmission within our definable environmental area. However, it is obvious that the voice entities are beyond our defined empirical level. Something that is observable through the medium of a tape recorder is no longer supernatural, it exists in conformity with certain natural laws; its production occures within defined possibilities of such laws although these possibilities might never have been explored before. We do not have to change our basic conception of physical laws to experience these voices. Our task is now to define the points at which they materialise. Apart from the serious scientific critic whom we must and can satisfy as to the existence of the voices, the more general criticism I have encountered is usually motivated by a genuine lack of religious faith; there is a paradox of belief within many people who are prepared to base their faith upon something completely above and beyond themselves, but who are not prepared to accept evidence which would show concretely that there is a type of existence different from our own. Anything that does not show the trappings of a heavenly appearance or confirm an after-life according to their own imagination is not acceptable to them. Deep down they are terrified to accept the rather serious implications of such evidence. Their entire thinking is guided by the 'here and now' which clouds their every thought of an after-life."

The research conducted by Mr. Prescott and the RTE technicians must be considered an important contribution towards a better understanding of the Voice Phenomenon. The rôle of Telefís Eireann, and especially the *Late Late Show*, in presenting the Phenomenon in such an objective way to their millions of viewers, must be considered a 'breakthrough' in its own right.

10

A Voice in the Wilderness

Away from the dramatic events which accompanied Raudive's book and the subsequent television and press publicity, David Ellis, M.A., pursued his own investigation into the Phenomenon. Although I have made references to the background of his research, and particularly to his supervisor, Mr. J. H. Cutten, some of Ellis' observations are important in the context of the Phenomenon as a whole.

Mr. Ellis' terms of reference refer to the 'Raudive Voices'; his main concern has therfore been Dr. Raudive himself and the doctor's immediate collaborators.

David Ellis was elected to the Perrott-Warrick Studentship in June 1970 and took up work in October. The board of electors consists of Cambridge graduates who are interested in psychic research. The grant is in the region of £700 per annum, and Ellis has received the Studentship for two years. In January 1972, I interviewed him and these are his findings and opinions as I recorded them. After eighteen months of research, Ellis was convinced that the phenomenon is not as easily reproducible as Dr. Raudive tends to make out, and that the voices, if they are of para-normal origin, are not as frequent as Raudive believes. Of those voices which Ellis listened to during his three visits to Dr. Raudive, he believes a proportion is derived from normal radio sources. A small fraction, however, is in Ellis' opinion genuinely para-normal. He is reluctant to commit himself either way because he has found it practically impossible to distinguish between those which might be para-normal and those which he believes are not. His reservoir of research material consists of twelve or thirteen recordings, taped during his visit to Raudive in the autumn of 1971. He intends evaluating them by listening to them and noting the difference between his own interpretation and that given by Raudive. He then intends to play them to some friends and see whether they can hear them as well. If a given number of voices can be objectively heard, he still would have to make up his mind whether they are para-normal or not. How this could be achieved, he does not know at the moment. "However," he assured me, "there are still a few months to go". Ellis would be willing to accept the para-normal nature of voices if he could be certain that they were not freak pick-ups, and if all normal and natural causes could be excluded as reasons for the recording. He intends to devise a method which would enable him to distinguish between para-normal voices and others sufficiently easily, so that he could put forward a theory of which condition produces a genuine Phenomenon. So far he has not been able to conduct any research into this possibility but he hopes to do so.

Ellis' visit to Dr. Raudive has not yielded the expected results and solutions. He believes that not many of the voices obtained during the twelve short recordings are genuine. This assumption he bases on listening to the interpretations given to the voices by Raudive himself.

I then questioned David Ellis about Professor Bender's research and those voices which have been printed on a voice printer. He admits that there are voices but stresses that Professor Bender is very selective as to which voices he considers para-normal. Ellis also accepts that it only needs one single voice to be proved to be of para-normal origin to prove the case of the Voice Phenomenon, but he feels that he could have done so early on in his research if Dr. Raudive had agreed to come to England and experiment with him in a screened room. Basically, Ellis feels that his research of the Voice Phenomenon under the terms of his reference, "Raudive Voices", has been a handicap, largely because of the doctor's unpreparedness to come to England for experiments. Before going to Germany, Ellis had hoped to do one hundred recordings with Dr. Raudive; however, the doctor did not agree to this as he believed it was a foolish exercise just sitting there and recording for hours without making an analysis of the work. On the other hand, Ellis agreed that he had no knowledge of German, Latvian or Baltic languages which were likely to occur in any of Raudive's recordings, and only twelve recordings were made and analysed.

I pointed out to David Ellis, not as a criticism of his work but as a statement of fact, that the larger part of his preliminary reports only related to hearsay. I asked him whether it would not have been more advantageous for him to have concentrated on doing experiments for himself and acclimatising his hearing to the strange rhythm and frequency of those voices; this would have enabled him to make independent observations and interpretations from Dr. Raudive. "I do not agree with your suggestion," he answered "as I have said in my report No. 10, it is necessary to concentrate at this stage on Konstantin Raudive, firstly because it is he who is making these claims that he can obtain voices of the dead on tapes. Therefore one just goes to see what he gets on his tapes, rather than trying to get something on one's own tapes, which Raudive might claim is not what he gets at all. Another reason is that possibly mediumship may be involved if the Phenomenon is genuine. If I started to make experiment of my own, I might develop that kind of mediumship and receive a lot of good voices. If I then went and did experiments with other people, this would always certainly be a contributory factor, whether it was I who was the medium or what! A further reason is, if I started making recordings on my own without reference to what other people have done, on the Continent or elsewhere, then I would start where Raudive started in 1964 and Jürgenson started in 1959; at square one. It seems to me that these people have worked on it for better or for worse, for five years in Raudive's case and ten years in Jürgenson's. So I just find out what they have done rather than start at the beginning again."

I asked David Ellis whether he thought any progress had been made over the last two years. "I have my doubts, actually," he answered. "What I found extremely disappointing were the experiments people have not done; from reading Mr. Bearman's article one would imagine that scientists are busily trying to find out this and that. I think half the things they say that they have done, were not done but should have been done. I have found it very difficult to get details of any experiments at all."

This, Ellis stressed, did not apply to himself; he had not conducted experiments for the reasons mentioned earlier. "But," he continued, "I asked Dr. Raudive whether he had ever made a recording, using more than one tape recorder. I was told that there had been one occasion when four tape recorders were used at the same time. So I wrote to Professor Schneider and asked him for more details, and he wrote back to me saying that he had not done any such experiments and I should not place too much reliance on four tape recorders." (Actually, four tape recorders were in use during the Pye controlled test. Mr. Bearman was present and so was Dr. Raudive; Professor Schneider was at that time in Switzerland and knew nothing about these tests.)

In conclusion I asked David Ellis whether he had already formed an opinion about the Voice Phenomenon. I pointed out that he could not write a report and remain 'sitting on the fence'. "Most people do," he answered. "I have still some months to go and I don't think I should have a conclusion even at this stage. I am giving simply an interim conclusion which is that some of the voices might be genuine. What I have to do now is to show that some of them are genuine. I can then draw conclusions from the facts. But one has got to find out the facts first. It is obvious that some of the voices are definitely not genuine. For example there was one voice which Raudive got when we were there . . . . that was the first time I ever went. We were not actually present at the recording but Raudive had made this recording after we had left and he played it to us on the following day. In this recording, Raudive asked his friend Nimowald to speak to him in Russian. He switched to the Goniometer and after some time there was quite a sequence of voices which were preceded by a rather interesting comment which he interpreted as a voice saying that there was interference. When we came to this point of the tape, Raudive told us that there would be interference. Then came a voice and he interpreted it as 'glaube du Schidin'. Apparently Schidin was somebody who did not believe in the voices but does now; then came a Russian sentence, which I looked up in the Russian dictionary and it meant that Nimowald was exhausted to death. This gentleman Nimowald had actually been sent by the Russians to Siberia, and that was the last Raudive knew about him. At the end of the message, the voice said in Russian 'enough', and that was the end of a remarkable recording. I have always said if Raudive is wrong on other voices, he is right on this one, because I heard it quite clearly. On my last visit I got a copy of this recording because he is not very keen on parting with the original recordings. After my return to England, I played this voice to some friends in Cambridge. When they heard this sequence, they roared with laughter because they told me it was Radio Luxembourg I had on the tape. They are friends of Radio Luxembourg and a programme called 'Jensen's Dimensions' which comes on at one o'clock in the morning. I asked my friends what it normally said on that programme and they told me that it starts off with "Hello this is Kid Jensen' which Raudive thought is 'Glaube du Schidin'; 'reminding you about dimensions'—obviously that was where Raudive thought it said 'Romanov Nimowald', and so on. This recording was done on a goniometer."

I have never heard this programme on Radio Luxembourg, nor the recording made by Dr. Raudive. Ellis says in one of his reports: "Everyone, with the possible exception of Dr. Raudive himself, agreed that a major problem lies in the interpretation of the voices." This is certainly true, and if the above case quoted is correct, Dr. Raudive has been unwise to allow himself so much literary licence in interpreting the voices.

Under the studentship, David Ellis is obliged to write a paper of approximately 1000 words every six months. At the end of his studies, he will write an extended paper for the journal of the S.P.R.

To what extent Theodor Rudolph's goniometer provides a better or safer method of recording is a matter for future experiments to find out. Ellis seems to be impressed by the gadget; I have yet to be convinced that the radio/self-transmitter/microphone method is not far more likely to pick up random radio waves than, for example an ordinary diode.

Mr. Ellis has been very frank with me in discussing the work he has done and not done, and in explaining his own ideas. I believe his reasons for not conducting his own experiments to be wrong; moreover, they are certainly not logical or academically justifiable. His main objection to experimenting was that there might be mediumship involved and he saw a danger in developing it. Ellis must know that he will never be able to prove the existence of incipient mediumship in a person. Why then, does he base his excuse for his negligence on such a wild assumption? What he is really saying is that no researcher can possibly carry out a successful experiment without running the risk of developing mediumship which would automatically render his research invalid. Thus Professor Bender, Dr. Karger and everybody else who has recorded the Voice Phenomenon could be mediums, so their results must be ignored. It is an original idea, but the strangest excuse I have come across in my academic career. His other objection is Raudive, who has done six years of research: Ellis feels that he should investigate and judge what Raudive has done rather than conduct his own experiments because it would mean starting at the beginning again. I have always believed that any research must start at square one; in a true scientific investigation it is highly damaging to the investigator if he spends his time cutting corners and guessing. Thirdly, Ellis maintains that his prime task is to investigate Raudive, because the doctor claims to have established communication with the dead. I am afraid that this too is an illogical presumption on the student's part: his task is to investigate the claims and that means the voices as a whole. Ellis' main criticism is directed against Raudive's method of interpreting. He may have a good point here, but it is irrelevant and immaterial whether Raudive interprets correctly or not: what is important is to establish the origin of the voices.

Dr. Raudive cannot be blamed for refusing to come to England to be investigated. He may or may not have a high opinion of himself or even be contemptuous of those who do not agree with him; nevertheless, the onus is on the investigator to conduct his tests wherever Raudive consents to hold them. Two weeks after the publication of *Breakthrough*, one of the most popular magazines in Britain, *Woman's Own*, wanted to bring Dr. Raudive to London for an experiment with some of their readers. This would have given excellent publicity to the book, and in turn, additional royalties to the author. Dr. Raudive refused; he explained that he was exhausted and could not possibly make the journey again at the moment. He also told me that it was irrelevant to him whether a woman's magazine gave publicity to his work. Naturally I was disappointed but there was nothing we could do as publishers, although we stood far more to lose than David Ellis by Raudive's refusal to come to England.

In February 1972 Mr. Ellis published and distributed his preliminary Reports, nos. 7-12. Basically they contain the information he had given me in a recorded interview in January, however, some of the points and observations he makes deserve special mention.

Under the heading 'Publicity' (no. 7) he says: 'Mr. Peter Bander made a number of recorded broadcasts about the book in the north of England in April' and he frequently refers to a discussion on *Late Night Line-up* on April 26. Although there is no real need for him to mention the activities of a publisher at all I cannot help noticing that when he does so he tends to minimise everything that could be interpreted as a positive contribution to the study of the Phenomenon.

Another example may be found under the heading 'Information received' (sic) in no. 9 Ellis simply states: 'In a review of *'Breakthrough'* in the summer issue of *'Light'* Mr. Norman Gaythorpe said that a tape recorder, under suitable conditions, could pick up local telephone conversations as well as distant radio programmes.' Bearing in mind that this particular issue of *'Light'* gave a great deal of information of a technical and psychological character, offered by four separate correspondents (see Chapter 7), I must say I am amazed by Mr. Ellis' selective presentation of facts. He must surely have received information from Dr. Crookall, Mr. Bearman and Mr. Beard as well as from Mr. Gaythorpe: it was all in the same issue.

As Mr. Ellis has chosen to send out his research report diaries he must be prepared to accept criticism even before he has completed the term of his Studentship.

It is now obvious that the outcome of David Ellis' investigation will be neither startling; nor will it contribute new facts to the research in general, unless some miracle happens in the very near future. To debunk some of the things Raudive has said would be easy, but I don't expect Ellis to stoop to a personal attack. This leaves the problem of interpreting the voices, and a collection of interviews with people whom Ellis has visited, such as Mr. Philip Rogers of Grindleford, Sheffield, (Report no. 2) who has a large collection of recordings which he believes are derived from Unidentified Flying Objects; a Mr. and Mrs. X were interviewed by Ellis after they had a sitting with a medium which was recorded. Five experimental sessions were held at my own home, and Mr. Ellis might discuss them and, of course, comments from scientists and researchers. It remains to be seen whether the S.P.R. will hail Mr. Ellis' article or thesis as an authentically documented investigation into the 'Raudive Voices', giving a solution to the mystery. I am sure that Mr. Ellis has worked to the best of his ability, and his conclusions deserve to be published, if only for that reason. But they should be seen and judged in the same light as that in which Mr. Ellis sees the experiments of some of the Continental scientists: "much of what was said had been done, has not been done but ought to have been done."

I

11

The Scientists and the Voices

There has been a remarkable lack of any concerted effort
to present a comprehensive report on the development of
the Voice Phenomenon. Individual groups of scientists and
Institutes are actively engaged in research but it would be
wrong to speak of an inter-related network. The discoverer
of the Voice Phenomenon, Friedrich Jürgenson, is still
active in Sweden, Dr. Raudive experiments in Bad Krozingen, Germany, Professor Bender's University Institute
works in collaboration with Mr. Sotscheck's research group
in Berlin, Theodor Rudolph and Franz Seidl operate in
Southern Europe. In my introduction I contrasted the
approach to the Phenomenon in Britain and Ireland with
that in other European countries. It is therefore unlikely
that a concerted and joint report on the developments
within the various groups will be published in the foreseeable future. Individual reports and publications are now
appearing more frequently, and I cannot help feeling that
they are designed to persuade readers to adopt the one
or the other attitude to the Phenomena, rather than just
inform.

Shortly after *Breakthrough* had appeared, I received a
letter from a Swedish scientist. He complained that in Dr.
Raudive's book the vital part played by Friedrich
Jürgenson had been completely understated. Although I
knew of Mr. Jürgenson's existence, the extent of his work
and his present activities were unknown to me. I felt I

ought to write and explain to him the lack of information available to us before the publication of *Breakthrough*. During the same week, a journalist drew my attention to Jürgenson's close connections with the Vatican and Pope Paul VI in particular. It was also told that in 1969 the Pope had decorated Friedrich Jürgenson with the Commander's Cross of the Order of St. Gregory the Great and that cardinals and other members of the Vatican were acquainted with Jürgenson's discovery. Apart from pictorial evidence, which showed the Pope during an investiture, there is little to prove that the Vatican may be interested in the Phenomenon; besides, Jürgenson's work as a film producer has brought him into close contact with the leaders of the Catholic Church.

On 10 August 1971, I received Jürgenson's answer; in an eight page letter he explained his own position and also his relationship with Raudive, Bender and other scientists.

". . . . For the same reasons which moved you to write to me, I will answer your questions and will be absolutely frank with you. I beg you not to mis-understand me. Konstantin Raudive has been my friend and pupil. Therefore *I do not wish him harm in any way!* During the first years of our collaboration he was fully dedicated to our research. Unfortunately this relationship has changed; it was after one of my lectures in Freiburg, in October 1969, when I noticed signs of rivalry, a fact which was commented on by many friends who were present. To cut a long story short, it was only with the greatest difficulty and much persuasion that I could move the editor of the magazine *Sieben Tage*' not to write a very negative article about K. Raudive.

To me, the bridge to another dimension of life is far more important, not only for scientific but for human-itarian reasons; I shall never allow personal ambitions and egocentric tendencies in researchers to cast a shadow over the project as a whole.

I think it goes without saying that there are no such things as 'Raudive Voices'. Nor are there 'Jürgenson Voices'; there are simply voices, which I believe belong to post-mortal men or women, who, for the last twelve years, have been trying to build a bridge between two dimensions of life; they are motivated by compassion and understanding for us. I don't know how much is known in Britain about my work; during the first four years, following the discovery, my entire energy was given to obtaining more and more irrefutable evidence on tape. In 1963 and again in 1964 I reported my findings to conferences in Sweden. Since 1964 I work in closest collaboration with Professor Hans Bender of the University of Freiburg and Dr. Friedebert Karger of the Max Planck Institute in Munich. Both scientists have become my close personal friends. Professor Bender's last visit to my home from 18 to 24 July 1971, resulted in the formation of a research centre to be situated in Southern Europe. This plan is to be realised almost immediately. Unfortunately, Professor Bender is not inclined to entertain any collaboration with Dr. Raudive.

So far we have published two books, one of which has been published in Swedish: 'Voices from the Universe'. It is now out of print, and the other, 'Radio Contact with the Dead' has appeared in German and in Swedish."

Mr. Jürgenson then lists the various activities he has engaged in during the last few years and mentions the television films he has produced; among them is a documentary film about Pope Paul VI. He then continues:

"Besides, and perhaps it is the most important aspect, I have found a sympathetic ear for the Voice Phenomenon in the Vatican. I have won many wonderful friends among the leading figures in the Holy City. Today 'the bridge' stands firmly on its foundations."

Professor Bender's research is perhaps best known through the quarterly publication *Zeitschrift für Para-*

psychologie und Grenzgebiete der Psychologie, a magazine published by the University Institute of Freiburg. I mentioned earlier that our publishing house was expecting a major contribution from Professor Bender for inclusion in *Breakthrough* which had been promised by Dr. Raudive. It was only when we realised that Bender was not going to contribute his article to the book but intended publishing it separately, that we went to print. I have already given the summary of the article earlier on; the thesis is entitled: "To the Analysis of extraordinary voice phenomena on electro magnetic tape—Research experiments with recordings by Friedrich Jürgenson." (The article is in German and appeared in Volume 12 no. 4). Prefessor Bender's magazine is in my opinion, the best publication in the field of parapsychology; I regret that it does not appear simultaneously in the English language because it deserves the widest circulation.

Jochem Sotscheck's research with the voice printer appeared in the same number; the title is "About the possibilities of recognising sounds of speech", and it is subtitled "Concerning the usefulness of the Visible-Speech-Process and other methods in the analysis of 'voice recordings' on electro-magnetic tape".

After preliminary explanations about audiometric and technical details (pp 239—241), Sotscheck concerned himself with the Voice Phenomenon: "From the twelve test recordings of voices, which had been recorded by F. Jürgenson, Mölnbo, Sweden, it could be seen from the 'visible speech spectrogrammes' that the frequency range of those 'recordings' stretched between 200 Hz and 6—7 kHz, in fact the same range within which 'normal' voices would be recorded. The other signals which are peculiar to 'voice recordings' also appeared in this frequency range. Such spectrogrammes give a visual representation of voice or noise occurences in a three-dimensional form."

"For these experiments we used the spectrograph which belongs to Voice Print Laboratories. It has a 300 Hz wide stable filter, which by a scanning process acts as a 'frequency window' and which slowly scans the entire frequency range (25 Hz—1kHz) under examination. Within 80 seconds an analysis of any sound occurrence on a tape of 2.3 seconds length is completed."

Mr. Sotscheck goes on to explain that voices of women and children register between 220 Hz and 330 Hz while a man's voice would register between 120 Hz and 160 Hz; he was therefore able to identify the origin of the voices examined—at least distinguish between female and male voices. Of course he realises that any results of such tests are only valid if certain prerequisites are fulfilled; for example, voice characteristics which are similar or identical to 'normal' registered speech.

The article is fairly lengthy, highly technical and requires substantial knowledge in the field of electronics to be fully understood or its significance to be evaluated. I take it as a matter of course that a learned journal of a major university does not publish scientific data and information which are not verifiable. I do not presume to understand Sotscheck's thesis fully, I am not at all qualified in electronics and cannot comment on Sotscheck's data or discuss them in depth. From what I have read and translated I understand that the experiments have proved the voices to exist, and photographs of the analysed voice prints show quite clearly characteristics similar to photographs of voice prints with normal' speech. Nowhere in his article does Mr. Sotscheck offer an opinion on the origin or possible nature of the voices, nor does he comment on the speech content.

Perhaps, on a lighter note, I should mention that there is yet another relevant contribution in the same journal. The author is Dr. Rüdiger Herren, a lecturer at the Institute for Criminology and the Execution of State Prosecution. (I doubt whether there is a comparable institution anywhere else in the world, but in translation the Institute's name may sound more frightening than it really is.)

Dr. Herren does not comment on Professor Bender's or Mr. Sotscheck's research; instead he concerns himself with the desirability or undesirability, of allowing para-psychologists to practise by themselves: "As far as parapsychology is concerned, the kind which is practised and taught at certain universities may in some special criminal cases be used to procure an interdisciplinary collaboration between parapsychologists and socio-psychologists on the one hand and criminologists, criminal investigators and police experts on the other.

"The parapsychologist should be a specialist in the field of superstitions and the occult theories which mankind has developed in the course of time. He should be an expert in modern occult sub-cultures, such as secret circles, where the black mass is celebrated, with witchcraft and spiritistic practices. Similar to drug-cultures of the younger generation, such occult sub-cultures are escape routes for those people who cannot face rationalism and the pressure of the pluralistic industrial society. It is a well known fact that the activities of believers in the occult, such as clairvoyants, exorcists, spiritistic mediums and the like, are on the increase in our society and lead often to criminal activities."

"The criminal investigator can benefit from the inside knowledge of the parapsychologist in discovering the motive-logic in cases of murders committed for superstitious reasons. Apart from physicists and police doctors, parapsychologists may be consulted when investigating cases of 'water divining' 'cancer forming earth rays and the sale of useless protection equipment', 'medical charlatans', such as people who conduct 'absent healing' or even give a medical diagnosis from afar!

"What is most important is to recognise that a para-psychologist can do himself only good if, when dealing with mediums, spiritual sensitives, or psychographologists, he immediately consults an experienced criminal investigator."

I am afraid that all the scientists, psychologists and researchers who have investigated the Voice Phenomenon are in Dr. Herren's bad books. I don't know what the position of the German nationals is and whether their findings are any the less valid for not consulting the learned lecturer. I have been assured by a reliable source that Scotland Yard has no objections to not being consulted, nor do they think that our scientists would have done themselves any good, dialling 999 before every experiment with the Voice Phenomena.

The fact that Dr. Herren's article follows those by Professor Bender and his associates underlines perhaps the slightly different approach to psychic phenomena or the para-normal in Germany. Obviously, the author means well and tries to protect his country from charlatans and spiritual evil-doers, but I cannot help wondering what exactly would happen if such an article appeared in a British learned journal.

Dipl. Ing. Franz Seidl, a contributor to *Breakthrough*, has also published his own research findings. He calls it "The Phenomenon of Transcendental Voices". The 64 page booklet (pubished by Frech, Stuttgart) consists of voice samples recorded by the engineer and gives detailed instructions how to build a psychophone, including the data for the transistors, 24 resisters and 18 condensers needed for such an instrument. Some results obtained with Seidl's psychophone are given in *Breakthrough* with a diagram of the instrument. The method employed is a combination of radio/self-transmitter/microphone recording. The actual voices do not differ in quality, content or audibility from those obtained by other methods.

Dipl. Ing. Theodor Rudolph, the inventor of the goniometer, and Professor Alex Schneider, the physicist, still collaborate with Dr. Raudive and so do a number of professors and scientists from the United States and other countries.

When Dr. Raudive came to England for the first time in 1969, I had invited Mr. Malcolm Hughes to be present at the experiment; he was at the time a student at Oxford, reading Science and Education. By the time Raudive came again, Malcolm had moved to London as a research student in Psychology. Because he seemed to get on well with Dr.

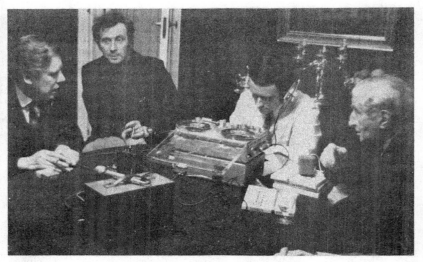

A controlled experiment was carried out by the chief engineers of Pye. The 18 minute recording yielded about two hundred voices of which twenty seven were clear enough to be played back over a loudspeaker. Four messages purported to come from Artur Schnabel, a life-long friend of Sir Robert Mayer. (l. to r.) the author, Ken Attwood and Ray Prickett (Pye), and Sir Robert Mayer.

During a series of experiments carried out by Leslie Hayward, a voice answered in response to the question what the best recording time would be: 'When the sun goes down'. (Leslie Hayward with David Ellis looking on)

Ralph Lovelock, physicist and electronics expert, believed as early as 1969 that the Voice Phenomena could probably not be explained by electronic means. Extensive tests proved him right.

Pan Collins, Senior Researcher, RTE, and programme adviser for the *Late Late Show*, recorded the first voices in Ireland. Gay Byrne, Producer/Compere of the Show, devoted two programmes to the Voices. A dramatic and controversial issue arose when one of the voices recorded by Mrs. Collins called out: 'Your mother, Gay, your mother." Telefis Eireann's presentation of the Voices has been largely responsible for the positive reactions from the Churches.

Colin Smythe, M.A., Publisher: "The term *Raudive Voices* is a misnomer. Raudive neither discovered them nor is he the only person doing experiments."

Ted Bonner, Decca and RTE: "This is no trick. This is no gimmickry; this is something we have never dreamed of before."

Following the publication of *Breakthrough*, Peter Bander appeared on twenty seven television and radio programmes. On *Late Night Line-Up* (BBC 2), he had his first public encounter with Spiritualists. Gordon Turner (centre) condemned the book as 'highly dangerous'. Rosalind Heywood, S.P.R., also participated in the discussion which was chaired by Sheridan Morley (left). During the debate it became clear that the Voice Phenomenon had to be presented independently from the book *Breakthrough*.

Michael Kaye: "If psychic manifestations take place in a different continuum then one is forced to speculate that they make use of different forms of energy as well."

Sir Robert Mayer, LL.D., D.Sc., Mus.D.: "If the experts are baffled, I consider this is a good enough reason for presenting the Voice Phenomenon to the general public."

Professor Dr. Hans Bender, University of Freiburg: "An examination with better technical equipment in May 1970 made the paranormal hypothesis of the origin of the Voice Phenomena highly probable."

Dr. Brendan McGann, Director, Institute of Psychology, Dublin: "I have apparently succeeded in reproducing the phenomenon. Voices have appeared on a tape which did not come from any known source."

Ken Attwood, Chief Engineer, Pye: "I have done everything in my power to break the mystery of the voices without success; the same applies to other experts. I suppose we must learn to accept them."

A. P. Hale, Physicist and Electronics Engineer: "In view of the tests carried out in a screened laboratory at my firm, I can not explain what happened in normal physical terms."

Raudive and also had been conducting his own experiments, I asked him to spend a week at my house and assist our visitor in his experiments and general needs. Malcolm Hughes was therefore closely in touch with the events, and I hoped that he could make a contribution to the research and tests carried out by Raudive in this country.

"I have accepted the fact that these voices exist and cannot be explained in normal physical or psychological terms", he told me a year later, after having conducted many more experiments by himself. "I must admit that I have found Raudive's method of experimentnig very trying and tedious; he is more intent on getting examples to add to his archives than on improving the quality of the voices and the clarity or suggesting a true interpretation; Raudive is certainly not as inquisitive or adventurous as I think he ought to be; he sticks to the same methods of recording and playback and, when discussing the subject, he insists on demonstrating what he has done rather than participate in a new venture.

"Personally, I would like to see the work done in collaboration with a medium; I feel that if it could be shown that the tape recorder and the medium receive parallel messages, verification of a sort would be possible. I am of the opinion that incipient mediumship is involved either as a detector or a catalyst; besides, I am sure that most, if not all, people possess a degree of mediumship.

"Dr. Raudive strongly denies the possibility of incipient mediumship being at least a part contributor to the Voice Phenomenon; I believe he is wrong and because of his stubbornness he makes it difficult for those who work with him to make a real contribution to the investigation. Apart from agreeing with him that a voice had manifested itself at a certain point on the tape, I often found myself in the position of disagreeing with his interpretations. Of course, it is reasonable to assume that some of the messages, at least those intended for him personally, are in a mixture of different languages, but he will do his utmost to persuade people that his interpretations are the right ones; there have been occasions when ten people heard clearly an English sentence or a name, and Raudive would insist that he alone could hear the true interpretation.

"There is something to be said for being confident, but I sincerely believe that Raudive's insistence has handicapped many experiments. I shall continue with my own experiments and especially on the lines I have mentioned with regard to collaboration with a medium."

No doubt, sometime in the near future, one of these experts or perhaps an amateur enthusiast, will produce an instrument or modify his tape recorder, which will make it possible to hold a dialogue with the 'voices'. 'Dial M for Mother' sounds facetious or utopian if applied to the present state of research. It is still very much a question of pot luck whether or not voices manifest themselves, and when they do, we don't always know who they are or purport to be. More often than not, they identify themselves or give the name of the person for whom the 'message' is intended, but the poor quality is, as Bishop Butler said, "very much like a badly connected transatlantic telephone voice".

Why some people hear these voices and others don't may be explained medically; there are degrees of deafness to certain sounds and frequency ranges. Why some people can record voices on tape and others cannot is more difficult to explain. Whether psychic magnetism, mediumship, a psychological attitude at the time of recording or similar factors are important, I don't know, and it is possible that one or all of them contribute to the quality of the recording. In *Breakthrough* Dr. Konstantin Raudive has exhausted the present pool of human knowledge; it is a difficult book to read from cover to cover ; it contains thousands of examples recorded with all known recording methods. Technical data are supplied and scientific reports added. Many smaller reports by other experimenters have been included and an appendix with observer reports. It is by any standard the most comprehensive book on the research into the Voice Phenomenon available. Professor

Paul Keller put it in a nutshell:

"It is a revolutionary book full of the most sensational facts. I agree, all this must strike you as a little beyond comprehension, but it is reality. Read this book, read it three times."

In between the categories of the professional expert researcher on one side and the enthusiastic lay researcher on the other, is that rare breed: the neutral observer. The age of specialisation which started with the Industrial Revolution has left little room for those who can view and judge the incredible advance of science in relationship to the philosophy, religion and spiritual development of man. The sheer wealth of knowledge required in any single discipline of science reduces the general knowledge of the scientist in proportion to the advance made in his particular discipline.

Over the last ten years we have seen the continuing disappearance of the general practitioner and family doctor; group practices allow them to specialise in different branches of medicine and offer their patients expert treatment. The heart specialist of ten years ago, is outmoded; today we go and see a cardiographer and probably two or three specialists, each dealing expertly with one minute aspect of the heart's function. I am quoting this example because it lies within our personal experience. The average person knows little about the degree of specialisation that goes on nowadays in the academic and scientific worlds. Students going up to Oxbridge to read history, specialise almost from their first year in a relatively short period of history. In order to acquire a more comprehensive picture of man's past, books are prescribed to fill in the background. Physics and electronics are beset by the same problems. Psychology has been divided into many self-contained sub-disciplines of which parapsychology is one, but the subjects and phenomena which interest the parapsychologist are so varied and far apart that further specialisation and subdivisions are the only solution.

Dr. Raudive's dilemma has been that he has tried to be

expert, researcher, philosopher, psychologist and objective interpreter of the Voice Phenomenon. It has been my contention for some time that his vested interest in the Voices and his personal involvement in the Phenomenon prevent him from being objective. He set himself the task to prove that the Voices were there: objectively speaking, he has proved this only to himself. When the Voice Phenomenon was introduced to Britain, Richard Sheargold made it clear that any claim of Raudive would depend for its success on the ability of others to obtain similar results using similar methods. (see Chapter 12). The electronic experts who were consulted have testified that the Phenomenon could not be explained in normal physical terms; in other words they were baffled. The psychologists have put forward an alternative theory which, however, would be far more difficult to prove than Raudive's claim that the voices are from the dead. The Church has accepted that voices from the dead do not contradict religious thinking and doctrine. The Spiritualists have acknowledged the post-mortal origin of the voices but differ greatly in their attitude to them. Researchers, both experts and laymen, have repeated Raudive's experiments and obtained results—electronic voices—and so the circle begins once again. Electronic experts will still be baffled, psychologists will go on examining aspects of the human mind in connection with the Voices, the Church will continue to reserve her judgement and Spiritualists will go on saying that the messages received through mediums are more coherent, clear and meaningful to the enquirer.

I said at the outset of the book that I am stock-taking and putting on record what is known about the Phenomenon, the people involved in it and the attitudes of interested parties. My report on the enthusiastic laymen is yet to come, but on reaching the summary on the experts and having looked at the attitude of the Church and the Spiritualists, I wonder whether this is not the place to break away for a moment from tape recorders, amplifiers, pulpits and seance rooms, and take a look at this whole

Phenomenon as it is seen by those who have retained the qualities of the true observer. No such person has come forward to offer his views; but then, getting involved in an issue would be contrary to their nature and position. I had to go out and find an observer's view, a task not dissimilar from finding an arbiter. The ideal person would be the one who could occupy a university chair in common sense, something which has yet to be established. His knowledge of electronics and psychology should match his logic and ability to draw from a wealth of experience and facts; this presupposes an unusually retentive memory and the ability to express any observation in a manner that can be clearly understood by all, the experts and the laymen.

Within most people's circle of acquaintances is probably a person who, to a larger or lesser degree, possesses such qualities. (I must be careful in what I say, because many of my friends consider themselves qualified within those terms of reference and they may be wondering why I did not solicit their opinion.) I am confident that the observations made by Mr. Michael Kaye express a concept of the Voice Phenomenon which will be welcomed by many. He examines the most fundamental question: "Is it at all conceivable that the voices have their origin outside possible electronic explanations?"

Michael Kaye has read *Breakthrough* and considered the evidence, theories and hypotheses concerning the Voices which are available at present. He began with an examination of one particular Voice Phenomenon which he had personally observed over a period of time. However, I restrict my report to a summary of his conclusions:

"Those who experiment with sophisticated electronic equipment will soon realise that the most unusual phenomena manifest themselves; for example, freak transmissions are sometimes recorded which have no right to be there, because the apparatus is not equipped to receive them. Until I read about the Voice Phenomenon of Raudive and others, I have always assumed that such freak recordings could all be explained electronically. I doubt whether tests and experiments to eliminate occasional voice manifestations have ever been conducted before the question of their origin was seriously challenged. The most obvious explanation which comes to my mind is that such voices are picked up because of a non-linearity in the circuits, which is acting as a detector stage. As far as I can see, this is still the only rational and logical explanation if the Voices are to be solved electronically. It would be foolish to shut one's mind to an alternative explanation, but naturally this is the simplest and first solution which occurs to me."

"I have theories of my own regarding psychic phenomena and, although I have never discussed them before, the recent controversy about a possible psychic origin of the Voices, has caused me to re-examine them. If you approach a psychic phenomenon, a poltergeist, a haunting, or any other, and do so in a rational manner, you look for elements which are common to them all; later you attempt to extract some generalities from a great number of peculiarities. It appears to me that one of the common factors which has been repeated about most psychic phenomena is the feeling of coldness when a manifestation is about to take place, and the focussing of the manifestation around a particular geographical location. Investigators who have reported such phenomena are quite precise in pointing to a locality. Manifestations are rarely reported taking place in ' a house' or in 'a large area', but 'up there on the third step down from the top' or 'down here in the left-hand corner' and so on. It has always appeared to me that if there is 'a will'—I am using this word for want of a better one—which is producing the manifestation, operating in some different continuum, and determined to make itself felt, perceived or heard in our space-time, it must avail itself of energy, because the only things we are equipped to feel, see or hear, are energy manifestations;

it does not matter what kind of energy, sound, electrical or sensory. It has always seemed logical to me that any 'jump' across from one continuum into another can only be achieved by whatever may be causing it, if it avails itself of thermal energy, and hence causes a drop in temperature; in other words, extracts energy from the ambient to manifest itself in some positive way. It therefore seems logical that such a phenomenon should be accompanied by a lowering of temperature.

"In the case of electronic voices, my reasoning is similar, but before explaining it I must stress that I am thoroughly agnostic in my attitude to them. I have neither accepted them as a psychic phenomenon nor rejected them as such. My mind is open to conviction but I am by no means convinced. If you accept that there is a will that is trying to achieve some form of communication, it is perfectly logical that one way of achieving it is the modulation of electrical fields or currents. Then you must ask yourself where, in this space-time continuum, is energy abstracted to make the modulation possible. It is interesting to reflect that if a voice were impressing itself electro-magnetically, on an existing circuit, it could either use the energy in that circuit or free electro-magnetic energy which might be present in the ether. The amount of energy required to modulate an audio-circuit is minute, compared with the total energy flowing through which manifests itself as waste heat; but an alternative is also possible, (if such voices are possible), and that is the great amount of free energy from radio broadcasts. Let me just illustrate this; before the war, a gentleman who lived in Hamburg, next to the transmitter of the radio station, managed to light his whole house with the energy radiated by the Hamburg transmitter; needless to say, that was quite illegal, but it can be done. If so much radiated energy is present, we only have to think of the many television and radio transmitters which are operating all the time, or as far as random radiation is concerned, powerlines etc., it seems to me quite an attractive thought that here is a free source of energy for anybody or any non-body who wants to make use of it.

"I have often wondered, and again assuming that psychic phenomena do happen, whether the catalyst, which is usually supplied by a medium, in assisting such phenomena to occur, is in fact an energy transformation circuit, sometimes assisted by other people. I have considered the possibility of, say, a ouija board, which requires group activity, being really a form of psychic circuit which acts as a rectifying circuit and a mechanism for energy transformation. If psychic phenomena exist, then I am forced to believe that they do so outside our space-time continuum and outside our energy relationships. There has to be a bridge between the two continua, and I wonder whether the concentration in a circle by holding of hands does not act as a circuit. (One is always tempted to say an electrical circuit, but psychic circuit would be more appropriate here.) The only function of such a circuit would be to build a bridge to the other continuum.

"Many of the psychic phenomena I have read accounts of including the Voice Phenomenon, make sense within the scientific framework of 'laws' we have established. Those manifestations do not contradict our limited understanding and they could only happen in the way they do.

"The moment you start reasoning about psychic phenomena, you enter the realm of 'energy relationships'. They take no account of distance or normal time relationships, and one is led to the conclusion that if there is another form of existence, it only touches our own at certain points and does not run alongside continuously. If the time scale is distorted or askew then one would also expect its energy relationships to be similarly distorted from our energy relationships, just as psychic time is askew in relation to 'real' time. What we are searching for is a formula to transform one to the other. It is almost like a formula for a Lorentz Transformation or a Fitzgerald Contraction; it does have a relationship to things that are happening in other velocities and other continua, but you have to have the formula before you can translate the one into the other.

"Because the Voice Phenomena are so random in their occurrence, so occasional in their perception, it is difficult to obtain enough 'raw material' from which to contruct a theory or a mathematical relationship, which, I am sure, does exist.

"If psychic manifestations take place in a different continuum, then one is forced to speculate that they make use of different forms of energy as well. After all, our experiences are human and terrestrial, and we are talking here of the extra-human and the extra-terrestrial; it is therefore reasonable to concede that there are other forms of energy and time relationships involved.

"If I believe that the physical world in which I live and which I think I can see, is really an artifact of my own mind, attempting to create a concrete model from energy and space relationships, then I can conceive of another universe with different energy and space relationships, in which 5,000,000 miles of our space is only an inch in a different continuum; therefore I would not necessarily need as much energy to cover that distance if I have the right transformation.

"One can look at this from both ways; if I say that I am now driving in my car from Gerrards Cross to Woodford, everybody understands what I am doing. But, what I am really saying is "I am transforming hydro-carbon oil into a different state to achieve expenditure of energy to operate on the mass of my being in order to transform it to a different energy

J

level, which conveniently I call Woodford. Our brain can comprehend Woodford and Gerrards Cross because we are, after all, a mixture of a hunting and agrarian animal, and this is a convenient way for our minds to work. Similarly it is easier for a hunter to get an arrow from him to a wild buffalo by constructing an idea of space from energy relationships, rather than to work it out mathematically. It is simply a convenience, a translation; it enables our mind to deal with things as does an analogue computer which, if we make a special effort, can carry out the functions of a digital computer. Our minds happen to be primarily analogue computers. If I pick up a parcel, it occurs to me that it is heavy and appears to have a certain mass and gravity. I cannot tell how much it weighs in pounds or kilos because my mind does not work digitally but in an analogue fashion. Therfore I know and register that this parcel is heavier than, say, my wallet; I establish an analogue relationship and not a digital one.

"Our minds attempt always to translate in an analogue form what is essentially digital in the Universe. Therefore if something is digital, it is susceptible of treatment by mathematical modes. There may well be another mathematics which touches ours at different points and it is simply a question of finding the formula. If mediums or clairvoyants who attempt to deal with psychic phenomena do so in their analogue form, they may simply achieve what is in fact a mathematical relationship between this Universe that we apprehend and another one which we barely apprehend. The same applies to the Voice Phenomenon; we are not reaching out for anything special but for something that is there all the time.

"All the research carried out in this field is merely an attempt at constructing the right network and the right circuit."

In his Chapter I under the heading (*ii*) *the theory of*

relativity, on page 9, Konstantin Raudive has put forward a theory which has caused scientists and philosophers to attack his logic and laymen to be utterly confused. He introduced the concept of an 'anti-world'; starting from the premise that he has proved the voices to be from the dead; he describes them as an 'objective reality' and concludes: 'The reality is the continued existence of our soul after death.'

Having had the opportunity of discussing this theory with Dr. Raudive, I formed the impression that he takes too many matters for granted as proved. Professor Powell of Queen's University, Belfast, based his eloquent attack on Raudive's 'sweeping statements' for which, the Professor explained, the author had no evidence. For example, Raudive says: "It is a well known fact that man has the innate ability to act upon matter without physical action; this psychic faculty is known as telekenesis." He describes his investigation as an 'empirically provable reality with a factual background'. Dr. McGann, the Director of the Institute of Psychology in Dublin, is equally unhappy about Raudive's assumptions which he presents as proven facts often without giving details of how he arrived at them. None of the leading psychologists and scientists, even Professor Bender, Dr. Karger and their German colleagues, have categorically stated that Raudive's theories are entirely wrong; they have only objected to his manner of presentation and unfortunate habit of making out that he has solved the mysteries of God, Man and the Universe!

A theory of relationships is obviously the first step to a solution of the mystery that surrounds the Voice Phenomena. It is therefore of great interest to see that Michael Kaye views the feasibility or possibility of the Voice Phenomenon being of psychic origin entirely from a theory of relationships. I am particularly happy about the way in which Mr. Kaye has explained the theory; the reasoning and logic is within the layman's ability to follow which, I do admit, was not always possible in Dr. Raudive's chapter on the theory of relativity.

It is therefore the task of experts, in the fields both of electronics and psychology, to find the formula of transformation. This leaves the amateur to experiment in his own way which, to quote Arthur C. Clarke, 'is probably nearer the truth both in the long run and in the short run.'

Kenneth Attwood, the Chief Engineer of Pye, who must be counted among the experts, endorses Clarke's law; after a long series of systematic trials and pre-determined experiments, he now puts forward the view that a solution might be found quicker by 'trial and error' experiments. Using Michael Kaye's terms, this would mean that the data supplied by the 'analogue computer' will be transformed into digital information instead of the other way round.

The race between the experts and the amateurs will, no doubt, create a spirit of competition, but neither of them can afford to ignore the other.

12

The Enthusiastic Amateurs

Arthur C. Clarke's comment on scientific discoveries and their development has much to commend it; however, it is not altogether true that ignorant enthusiasm about a scientific problem is enough to solve it. If this were so, the mystery of the Voice Phenomenon would have been broken within a few weeks. I never realised how many thousands of enthusiastic amateurs had taken up the challenge of the mystery voices.

I have lost count of the hundreds of letters we received, partly in answer to radio or T.V. programmes, partly as a reaction to my Preface in Raudive's book, and a great number in response to newspaper articles. The majority of letter writers wanted to know any short cuts to get voices quickly. Some enthusiasts had already organised parties at which 'voices from the dead' were planned as a special bonus for the guests. Many letters contained useful information; wherever possible we passed the correspondence on to the experts for evaluation.

We were also inundated with telephone calls and visits; the main part of this invasion died down after June 1971. Naturally, we have made new friends, and I am afraid, some enemies as well. About fifty manuscripts were sent or delivered by hand, all of which concerned 'spirit writings', or messages received by a variety of contraptions. At least ten writers claimed to be natural receivers of messages (as distinct from mediums and clairvoyants) as they only had to sit in certain chairs, touch a lawnmower or, in one case, visit a local convenience for gentlemen, and voices would manifest themselves. One persistent writer sent us ten-page letters, at a time, containing 'revelations about the obscenities committed by his neighbours and revealed to him by 'voices'. Many expected us to publish their books and told us that their discovery was superior to the Phenomenon we had described in *Breakthrough*. A few writers threatened to tell their own familiar spirits to upset our future experiments, unless, of course, we published their manuscript, and Gordon Turner received over fifty threatening letters and telephone calls after his comments on television about the 'link between fascism, black magic and contact with impersonating earthbound entities who deliberately delude and pervert others.'

I believe it is necessary to mention these fringe reactions; after all, they have been part of my experience.

It is impossible to estimate how many people have carried out experiments after reading Raudive's book, and subsequently told us about their successes and failures. Their letters have been helpful because the information received confirmed that the Phenomenon is not restricted to scientists with elaborate equipment. I mentioned earlier the recordings made by Mrs. Pan Collins, the Senior Researcher of RTE's *Late Late Show;* she had only used a small portable Philips recorder for her first attempt. Mr. Peter Prescott and a doctor friend have joined Mrs. Collins with more elaborate equipment. It appears that the later results are positive but qualitatively no better than those recorded on the smaller machine. I had the opportunity of discussing the recording technique with them and, in my opinion, sophisticated equipment may help in the playback but is immaterial to the recording of voices. One of the RTE technicians has developed a small diode with exchangeable aerials (6 cm, 8 cm and 10 cm). The whole gadget is about as large as a matchbox; the voices obtained with it are 'b' and 'c' quality on the Raudive scale. What has been important is the collaboration and constant exchange of ideas between the Dublin researchers; largely due to Mrs. Collins' popularity, she has had no difficulty in finding a circle of interested friends, all of whom are trying to be enthusiastic laymen in the spirit of Clarke's 'law'. I would not be surprised if the next breakthrough comes from Ireland because the approach there has been more concerted and their experiments more varied in character. The question of patience comes into this as well, and it is interesting that they are not looking for anything specific but endeavour to 'get the feel' of the Phenomenon rather than sensational results which are difficult to repeat.

Dr. D. R. Nanji of Göteborg in Sweden has written to us and visited Colin Smythe. Although well acquainted with technical and electronic matters, Dr. Nanji approaches the voices entirely from a Spiritualist's point of view. After reading the intermediate reports by David Ellis, which we had sent him, he wrote: "Unfortunately, the reports are not very helpful, and my own reaction is that one should avoid complicating the Phenomenon with too many gadgets. The type of microphone one uses has a profound influence on the results, especially those with sensitivity as low as 5 Hz, compared with the ordinary microphone (50—60 Hz)". What makes Dr. Nanji's information specially interesting, is that he appears to have received instructions for the use of electronic equipment through the direct voice mediumship of Mr. Leslie Flint. He was told by his wife (who died some time ago) that she would speak to him on a frequency in the shortwave band 7.07 (42.4 meters). Dr. Nanji's wish is to communicate with his wife directly; he intends to establish a proper radio contact which will enable him to hold a two-sided conversation. This, of course, brings us back to 'dial M for Mother'. I am anxiously awaiting his results because he was the only correspondent who told us of information received from or through a medium which might throw light on the matter.

Francis M. G. Morton of London questioned his beginner's luck when he received 'b' and 'c' voices during his first recording. Mr. Morton is obviously no stranger to

electronics because his suggestions for improving communication are beyond my knowledge or understanding. "I hope
to explore the lower frequencies through audio, ultrasonic
and radio frequencies; I may also try experimenting in the
infra-red regions with the aid of Gallium Arsenide
components; however, success in this region would be
unlikely, but it is worth a try." It was the last sentence
"it is worth a try", which struck me as the most important.
Again, I am looking forward to hearing about the results,
even if they are negative; Mr. Morton will have contributed
to the research by processes of elimination.

By far the most meticulous research record I have seen
to date has been compiled by Michael G. F. Taunton of
London. I have listened to many of his voice recordings;
some may be environmental sounds which were picked up
by the microphone, but others have all the characteristics
of Voice Phenomena. With microphone recordings one can
never be sure if one has not been present during the actual
recording, but with diode voices it is relatively easy to
distinguish, especially if the quality is good. Michael
Taunton's recordings contain a number of 'a' voices. They
are clear and there is no doubt as to what they say. He uses
a Philips recorder '4307', four-track and EMI tapes. He
records for periods of five to ten minutes at different times
during the day and evening. On average he gets one voice
every ten seconds. His log book is a model for any research
student! Apart from technical data, time, revolution
number on the counter, etc., he gives other relevant details
such as weather conditions, and he lists all the questions
he has asked, opposite the recorded voices. Each recording
session is followed by analysis of possible interpretations
of the voices received and a conclusion as to their relevance
to the questions asked. If ever a person deserved to be
given a studentship or a grant for psychic research, it is
Michael Taunton, and I sincerely hope that his qualifications (O-level G.C.E. only), will not bar him. In my years
as a tutor of students with excellent paper qualifications,
I have rarely seen such meticulous research records.

In August 1971 I arranged several meetings with Michael Taunton. Apart from the 'usual' voices, calling out names or commenting on things happening in the room, Mr. Taunton introduced a new aspect which needed most careful investigation and an immediate decision. For reasons still unknown to me, and in fact unknown in the history of the Voice Phenomenon, he maintains that his voices have adopted a threatening and menacing tone. I was unable, at the time, to find a single voice of the character described by him. However, I could only spend two three hour periods with him and his recording equipment. From past experience I know that this is not sufficient to endorse or reject his claims. Because of the overall impression I had formed about him and his research, I had no reason to reject his fears outright, and I suggested that it would be far better if he suspended all further experiments for a period of at least three months or longer. On 12 January 1972, I telephoned Mr. Taunton; he told me that he had started a new series of experiments in the first week of January, after a break of several months.

The only voices he has been able to record purport to stop him from experimenting. Notable among them are those saying: "stop recording" and "go away". Mr. Taunton is neither dismayed nor discouraged; he intends to continue and, as he says, "break their resistance".

He believes that he may be able to identify the origin of the voices recorded by him in the not too distant future, and adds: "I have, of course, my own theory of what the voice entities are, but I think it is too early to discuss this at the moment."

Not quite as dramatic in content, but nevertheless ususual are the voices Mr. Len Ingle reported from Manchester. He records usually between 1 a.m. and 2 a.m.; and the voices are frequent. His Christian name is called out regularly, and he recorded a voice purporting to be that of a close friend, within a few hours after his death. Mr. Ingle feels that he tunes into two different dimensions, depending on the technique he uses, or change of diode. Like some other experimenters, he appears to get a clicking noise in between the voices. Among the clear and audible messages are—"Is this a ouija board?"—"help me"—she's harmless"—"let go".

Both Taunton and Ingle appear to record voices of a completely detached nature, with the exception of Ingle's friend who is purported to have come through immediately after his death. Ingle's voice recordings have the 'lower astral' quality Gordon Turner is worried about; Taunton, if he is right, seems to link up with an even lower level, which is also mentioned by Turner. Only a very few of Raudive's recordings are on that level. It may therefore be possible that in certain circumstances voices are received which are undesirable. Seen in proportion, such recordings seem to be very rare indeed. Why Mr. Taunton and Mr. Ingle should have been singled out for receiving mainly undesirable voices, I don't know.

According to Colin Smythe, the cause may be a coincidence; he believes that individual tape recorders could act as a transformation circuit which, quite accidentally, serves predominantly a specific range of voice entities.

This may be so, I don't know; but there is little doubt that voices purporting to come from those with whom we have had a strong affinity during their lifetime make up by far the largest proportion of all recorded voices. This suggests that love or affinity are stronger than the accidental frequency 'preference' of the tape recorder.

Another explanation was offered by Leslie Hayward, who feels that the experimenter creates his own frequency range; in other words, establishes a subconscious link with voices operating within a limited field. Hayward's suggestion is, of course, very close to Professor Bender's animistic theory.

I have already said that psychological attitudes, incipient mediumistic gifts or subconscious factors might contribute to the quality of voice recordings; is it not also possible that personality qualities, as opposed to incipient mediumship, could influence the type of voice entity which manifests itself on tape? Michael Kaye mentioned different energy relationships in another continuum; is it not feasible that there is also a psychic polarity, as opposed to human relationships, which occasionally breaks into our dimension and results in recordings as reported by Taunton and Ingle? As Mr. Ingle mentions that he only tunes into this 'dimension' when using a specific recording method, it is obvious that he could avoid such recordings if he chose to do so. In the case of Mr. Taunton, I have wondered for some time whether environmental influences might cause the hostile voices. I am, however, not as yet convinced that the voices he refers to are really hostile. Should he, however, be satisfied that he is recording some kind of electronic poltergeist, I would suggest he leaves him strictly alone, as in that case further experiments would be a waste of time.

If the will of the experimenter can determine the voice contact, Mr. W. Greenfield, a Fellow of the Institute of Linguists, may well achieve results in his attempt to narrow down investigations to a single source or incident. He believes that an incident such as the Katyn murders ought to be 'tapped' so as to elicit information about this historical mystery. As there has been a concentration of similar experiences suffered by five thousand men, it might be possible, in his opinion, to carry out successful experiments by trying to link up with them. Mr. Greenfield must, of course, be aware of the danger such an experiment would carry: the temptation to interpret electronic voices, received in relation to the leading questions, would render the evidence unacceptable to many scientists. After more than two years of active involvement in the Voice Phenomenon, I have yet to come across any experimenter who has at will tuned into a particular voice if there was no link of affinity. My own experience, when the voices of my parents purported to answer, has never been repeated because I felt uneasy about the result. I have often tried to analyse what I had heard and what I probably expected to hear, subconsciously. Of course, what was so striking was the *characteristic* response which I immediately associated with my parents. If, therefore, the response was characteristic, was it not possible that the answer was expected? I certainly do not wish to decry Mr. Greenfield's suggestion but I wonder whether a real purpose would be served, apart from the academic exercise of such an experiment.

Dr. C. S. Nicholson, a member of the College of Psychic Studies, has concerned herself with voice content. She has drawn attention to the frantic attempts on the part of interpreters to make voices 'fit' the purported originators. Perhaps the best known example of all voices recorded is the one attributed to Sir Winston Churchill. J. C. Burley, M.I.Mech.E., had opened the controversy by stating: ". . . . the message purporting to come from Winston Churchill, according to the book, page xxiii and the commentary on the record, said 'Mark you, make believe, my dear, yes' but to my ears he is quoting a line from Elgar's Land of Hope and Glory, thus: 'Mark you, make thee mightier yet'. *This is a typical Churchillian mode of speech."* Gordon Turner called the first interpretation: "one of the less important speeches of Churchill" and considered the second interpretation to be a better one. Apart from the purely technical process of establishing exactly what the voice said, by means of a voice printer, the only way to interpret this sentence is by hearing and associating. Of course, the second interpretation is more Churchillian, as we knew the man to talk in public. However, there are those who knew him more intimately. Dr. Nicholson explains that 'my dear', was Churchill's way of addressing all his friends and she suggests that it is wrong to opt for a particular interpretation just because it seems to be more acceptable by public consensus.

After the disappointing aspects regarding the Society for Psychical Research which I have mentioned earlier, it is only right that the last example I have chosen to illustrate the wide interest shown in the Voice Phenomenon should concern some of the work done within that organisation. In June 1971, we received the following communication: "As a member of the Society for Psychical Research, and Chairman of the Survival Joint Research Committee, I have studied with great interest Dr. Raudive's Breakthrough and the record of the voices. In addition, as an amateur transmitter of 40 years standing, I claim to possess a trained ear. At present I am endeavouring to record the voices on my own tape recorder, and at the moment of writing have held about a dozen abortive sessions using the microphone method. I am perfectly prepared later to use other methods such as the diode and radio, but I do feel that I should at least be able to achieve some success by the simpler microphone method. I have, of course, listened most intently, and I am reasonably certain that I am not missing voices.

"It surprises me greatly that the senior Pye engineers were able to arrange with a reporter for a demonstration and to obtain voices so readily. It is also very surprising that they knew that the voices they would receive would be loud enough for the reporter to hear as presumably *he* had not spent three months training! One does find oneself wondering if the ability to obtain voices does not depend on incipient mediumship. If this were so, it would be regrettable, as only a handful of people would be able to duplicate Raudive's work.

"As of course you know full well, any scientific claim depends for its success on the ability of others to obtain similar results using similar methods, and therefore as I see it, it is of the first importance to encourage experimental work in every way possible.
Yours sincerely,
Richard K. Sheargold"
On 4 August, Mr. Sheargold wrote:
"At the present, despite about twenty tests held over different periods of the day and in different rooms of the house, I have not heard anything whatever . . . ."
"Generally I may add that I am most keen on the whole matter, and I have little doubt that I can be of

assistance to other researchers. But all depends on being able to receive the voices myself. If this depends on some obscure form of incipient mediumship then this may not be possible."

In early September Mr. Sheargold visited Mr. Smythe and discussed possible improvements of recording and playback techniques. Colin Smythe suggested that earphones might help Mr. Sheargold to adjust his hearing more quickly; he was also able to demonstrate some of his own recordings both with and without the use of earphones.

Mr. Sheargold's letter of 20 September to Colin Smythe was, perhaps, the most gratifying communication we have received in connection with *Breakthrough*.

"My phones arrived and I heard my first voice the same evening—a male voice; practically interrupting my own voice—two words in characteristic rhythm and speed. The following evening I had one word only from apparently the same chap, but very weak indeed. I am so far quite unable to make out the words spoken, but by Raudive standard I suppose they were fairly loud. The next night seemed to be a blank, and then I knocked up a diode. I had several tests with it and got nothing. I switched off after the last test had been examined, but then decided to make sure that the diode was working correctly and switched on again just for a second or so. After this test I listened to that second or so when I had been messing around with the diode without saying anything myself, and I was amazed to find that a woman had spoken before I had had time to make any adjustments—immediately I had switched on in fact. She is the clearest and best voice I have had so far, and reasonably loud—also the longest—three syllables, but I still cannot understand what she said—it seems as though the consonants get lost. Practice may help. The funny thing is that this woman would hardly seem to be addressing herself to me, since I had made no announcement and in fact did not do so! But I am perfectly satisfied that it was a genuine phenomenon by the speed of utterance and the unmistakable rhythm.

"I could never have heard these voices so soon without the assistance you have given me, and I am most grateful—also for the loan of the Ellis papers which to me are most interesting. He is a lucky fellow to be able to devote so much time and energy to the work—I envy him. I notice that the last report is dated April—has he circulated any more, or is he too busy?

"Of course so far as I am concerned, this is only the beginning, although a very heartening one, and now I have begun I intend to go ahead; firstly by having more personal experience in hearing the voices. At least I am now in a position to assure my colleagues in the S.J.R.C. that the phenomenon is real!"

13

Carry on Talking

After the second *Late Late Show*, Terry Prone felt a little uneasy; she had told the audience that after the first programme she had realised that her initial belief that the 'voices' were from the dead, had been based on the wrong reasons. "Peter is so sincere, and he is a professor and such a good talker, that I just accepted what he said". Her objections against other speakers were based on similar grounds: Father Pistone for example, was another sincere man, who talked so well and put his points so clearly; yet Miss Prone felt that she should not trust us, just because we were sincere and could make a case for the voices. I think she was upset because she really did not want to offend us by asserting her right to disagree with our viewpoints.

Of course, I was not offended and neither was Father Pistone. However, this incident reflects a true picture of what goes on in many people's minds. I don't think that I or anybody else will ever be able to convince people, certainly not if their personal doubts keep on nagging them, and their own reasoning cannot lead them to a similar conclusion to mine.

My only answer is, and always has been, to suggest that they carry out their own experiments and find out for themselves whether or not the voices are there. Once they have recorded voices, it is up to the experimenter to make up his or her own mind whether these voices are random freak pick-ups, electronic impulses from the subconscious or, what has been suggested, a phenomenon which has led me to believe that their origin may be a post-mortal entity.

Recently, I have become a little impatient when friends or acquaintances wanted additional reassurance from me; I cannot understand why my personal opinion should make the voices any more real or define them as voices from the dead. I have stated many times that the Voice Phenomenon has neither changed my religious beliefs nor my way of life. Father Pistone said that the voices might be looked upon as confirmation, if such a confirmation was in fact needed, that there is a life after death. His beliefs and mine may well differ in some aspects, but I endorse wholeheartedly what he has said. Personally, I do not need the voices and I doubt whether I shall ever carry out an experiment to get a personal message; I feel that I don't need to establish such a communication. However, I appreciate that many people long for the opportunity of speaking to those whom they have lost; and as in most other aspects of life, one man's meat is the other man's poison.

I have written this book only because I believe it to be necessary to have a record of the Voice Phenomenon in the presentation of which, to millions of people, I have been materially involved. I feel responsible for keeping this record straight; if the evidence supplied by the experts and the results of experiments carried out by hundreds of scientists and laymen are convincing, then such a conviction is based on facts. I do not expect anybody to take my word for it that the Voice Phenomenon exists; those who have doubts about the origin of the voices, must consider the three main theories which have been put forward as alternatives. The fact that I have made up my own mind should neither prejudice nor influence the decision of a serious enquirer.

In the Preface to *Breakthrough*, I gave such information about the technical requirements and recording methods as I knew of at the time. I don't think I can add to them, because no new methods have been discovered in the last

K

year, and it is doubtful whether the tape recorder, as we know it, will ever yield better results than are achieved now.

The recordings manifest themselves on the electromagnetic tape, but nobody has discovered why and how the impulses get onto the tape. The methods of recording employed have been so different that we can rule out any of them being essential to the Voice Phenomenon. Several voices have been recorded on tape without a diode, microphone or similar transformer having been used; the recorder had been set on 'record' but nothing was connected to the input.

I can only offer some personal experience in playback, but I stress that I do so without claiming to be an authority in this subject.

Earlier in the book, I mention the tape loops; none of them has yielded better voices, on the contrary, not a single 'A' quality voice has ever been recorded on them. The size of the loop depends on the make of the tape recorder; using two empty spools, I threaded a piece of tape through the recording/playback head and followed the usual way of the recording tape, and with a piece of self-adhesive tape I stuck the two ends together. In the case of my Ferguson recorder, I needed 32 inches of tape. At a recording speed of 3.75 i.p.s. the loop took about $8\frac{1}{2}$ seconds to complete one revolution. Any message on the loop tape would therefore be repeated every $8\frac{1}{2}$ seconds, and I saved a great deal of time, which had been taken up with running the tape forwards and backwards when I wanted to hear a particular voice many times over. Such a loop has a serious drawback: one can only record for $8\frac{1}{2}$ seconds and it is by no means certain that a voice manifests itself, and on playback I have noticed several times that I appeared to have cut a voice off half way through the sentence because the $8\frac{1}{2}$ seconds were up. Nevertheless we have had a few good and relevant messages on loops and they can be of great use if one makes a loop of a passage on a tape which is proving difficult to interpret.

Generally speaking, for every minute of recording one

has to be prepared to spend fifteen minutes at least on the playback, often just to make certain that one is not mistaken in what one hears.

I have always found that the machine on which the recording is made need not be a very good or expensive tape recorder. As a matter of fact, I don't know of any make which has not produced voice recordings. For the playback it is different: the controls on a more sophisticated machine allow one to regulate the volume, bass, treble and, in the case of earphones being used, the amount of volume in the individual ear pieces. This does assist the researcher in adjusting his hearing more easily.

It is impossible to amplify the voices without amplifying the background noise as well. On the record which accompanied the Raudive book, each voice is repeated four times, but that is not all. By very carefully monitoring the original tape, the exact location of the voice was defined, and the small fraction of the tape with the voice on was isolated. This is a most time-consuming process and certainly not possible during ordinary playback.

The use of earphones helps but is by no means a guarantee for hearing the voices better; in fact, there have been recordings which could be heard far more clearly when they were amplified over a loudspeaker. It is difficult to explain why this is so. Basically, it is a problem of getting the voice separated from the background noise, the hissing of the tape and the frequent interferences. I suppose that every researcher has in time developed his own method of achieving a listening capacity. To me the noise resembles the sound of a waterfall between the speaker and myself. I therefore attempt to hear the voice above the noise.

The real problem lies in the interpretation of recorded voices. Most of the experts have commented on the difficulties, and David Ellis considers interpretation an insurmountable obstacle.

My own system, for want of a better one, is quite simple and straightforward. I prefer to conduct all playbacks when two or three or more people are present. Each of the listeners has his own set of earphones which are connected by means of a junction box to the output of the tape recorder. Everybody writes down what he hears; but it is important that they do not tell each other about their interpretations.

Personally, I seem to hear the vowel sounds first; I write these down. Others may hear consonants or even whole words, but I have also noticed that those who are in a hurry to get the whole message down immediately retract their opinion far more often than those who take their time over the interpretation. Quite frequently, the voice interpretation presents little difficulty. About half of the voices can be identified after six to ten playbacks; a quarter may take twenty playbacks or even thirty, the rest may take half an hour or longer, and usually there is disagreement on one or two of the words.

During the playbacks I make sure that the telephone does not ring. The shrill sound of bells usually ruins the playback for an hour or more. I have never known a disagreement on the type of voice heard: whether it is a man's or a woman's voice is easy enough to detect; even if it is an indifferent voice which qualifies for neither, the experimenters seem to agree on that.

There is, however, one aspect which puzzles me very much. I have neither enough 'raw material' to use in evidence nor am I at all sure that the isolated cases in question are what they appear to be. I simply put on record that during the last two years we have had five recordings which were interpreted by three or four experimenters, and the interpretations have been identical, with the notable difference that at least one of the interpreters had heard the sentence in German and the others had written down the same sentence in English or any combination of two different languages.

On replaying the dozens of voice samples Dr. Raudive had sent us for the gramophone record, I have found a large proportion of them which I believe to be different from his interpretation. But this is quite different: in his case, the problem of vocabulary, or lack of it, is the only possible explanation. In the five cases I mention, the meaning of the sentence is identical but the phonetics do not seem to match. There is, however, a similarity between the phonetics, such as 'dead' and 'tot', 'Mutter' and 'Mother', 'Vater' and 'Father', 'is' and 'ist', 'war' and 'was'. Words like 'here' and 'hier' are phonetically similar to a certain degree, and it would be impossible to differentiate between them on a voice recording.

It is therfore quite possible that some sentences could be heard in two languages, sounding *almost* the same. Still, it is just one of those things which complicate matters when one least expects or wants it.

Whether or not the mystery of the Voice Phenomenon will be broken in the near future remains to be seen. Until then, we can just hope that those who communicate provide us with more evidence and carry on talking!

Index

Catholic Church, *see* Roman Catholic Church
Catholic Parapsychologists, International Society of, 30, 47
Central Office for Telegraphic Technology, Berlin, *see* Telegraphic
    Technology, Central Office for,
Childers, Erskine, 40-41
Church Times, The, 90
Churches' Fellowship for Psychical and Spiritual Studies, *see* Psychical
    Research, Churches' Fellowship for,
Churchill, Sir Winston, 73, 74, 152
C.I.A., 57
Clarke, Arthur C., 69, 71, 143, 145, 147
College of Psychic Studies, *see* Psychic Studies, College of,
Collins, Mrs. Pan, 27, 105, 106, 107, 110, 112, 146, 147, ill.
C.P.S., *see* Psychic Studies, College of,
Crookall, Dr. Robert, 78-79, 124
Cross, Jennifer, 63
Cutten, J. H., 50, 51, 117

Daily Telegraph, The, 43, 69
Decca, 27, 105
De Chardin, Teilhard, 86
De Manio, Jack, 67, 74
Deavalow, Mrs. Y., 53
Dowding, Lord, 24
Duguid, Julian, 78, 79

Ellis, David, 15 ,35, 42, 43, 44, 47, 48, 49, 50, 51, 64, 65, 73, 117-125,
    147, 155, 159, ill.

Field Physics, German Institute for, 71
Flint, Leslie, 147
Fort, Charles, 87
Fowler, Mrs. Nadia, 21, 38, 47, 54, 74
Frei, Prof. Gebhard, 30, 31, 89, 91, ill.
Freiburg, University of, 14, 70, 126, 129

Gaythorpe, N., 78, 79, 124
German Institute for Field Physics, *see* Field Physics, German
    Institute for,
Goniometer, 48, 121, 122
Graham, Fergus, 112
Greenfield, W., 151, 152

Hale, Peter A., 64, 65, 66, 68, 70, ill.
Hayward, Leslie, 26, 35, 42, 47, 49, 107, 150, ill.
Heywood, Rosalind, 72, 73, 85
Heim, B., 71
Home Tonight, 93
Herren, Dr. Rüdiger, 130-132
Hughes, Malcolm, 53, 132-134